West Bank/East Bank

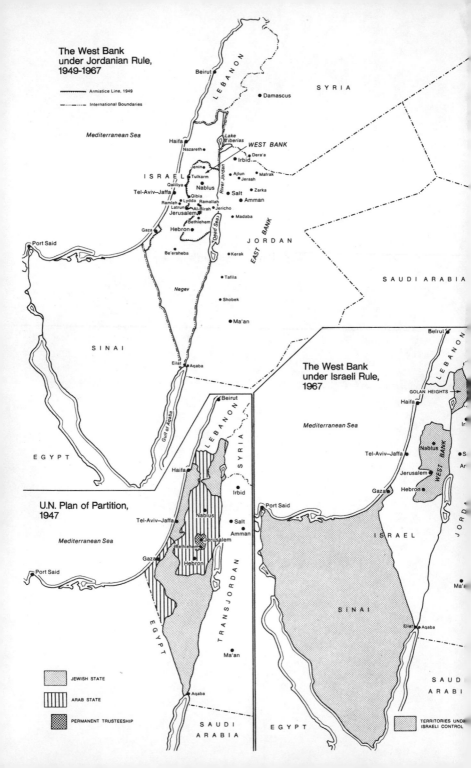

The West Bank
under Jordanian Rule,
1949-1967

········· Armistice Line, 1949

─·─·─· International Boundaries

The West Bank
under Israeli Rule,
1967

U.N. Plan of Partition,
1947

JEWISH STATE

ARAB STATE

PERMANENT TRUSTEESHIP

TERRITORIES UNDER
ISRAELI CONTROL

West Bank/East Bank

The Palestinians in Jordan, 1949–1967

Shaul Mishal

New Haven and London, Yale University Press, 1978

Designed by John O. C. McCrillis and set in IBM Press Roman
type.

Printed in the United States of America by The Murray Printing
Company, Westford, Massachusetts.

Published in Great Britain, Europe, Africa, and Asia (except Japan) by
Yale University Press, Ltd., London. Distributed in Australia and
New Zealand by Book & Film Services, Artarmon, N.S.W., Australia;
and in Japan by Harper & Row, Publishers, Tokyo Office.

Library of Congress Cataloging in Publication Data

Mishal, Shaul, 1945–
  West Bank/East Bank.

  Includes index.
  1. Palestinian Arabs—Jordan—Politics and government. 2. Jordan—
Politics and government.
  I. Title.
DS153.55.P34M57   323.1'19'27569405695   77-20692
ISBN 0-300-02191-7

For Rachelle

How narrow the space, how slight the chance
For civil pattern and importance
Between the watery vagueness and
The triviality of the sand,
How soon the lively trip is over
From loose craving to sharp aversion . . .
Remember that the fire and the ice
Are never more than one step away
From the temperate city: it is
But a moment to either.

From *Alonso to Ferdinand*
W. H. Auden

Contents

Preface

A few years ago, when I first became interested in the Palestinian issue, I was struck by the extent to which scholars' interests were shaped by current political events. Only after the Six-Day War was the term "Palestinians" reborn in the political dictionary of many countries, having been dead since the 1948 Arab-Israeli War. The same situation prevailed in the field of Palestinian studies. I found that scholars had written many volumes on the Palestinian Arab issue for the periods prior to 1948 and after 1967, but few researchers, except among the Palestinians themselves, had examined the events of the 1950s and often the 1960s.

Since 1967 the Palestinian issue has been a major and complex element pervading world politics. We must be careful, however, not to overstress its present aspects or allow them to overwhelm us. The major objective of this book is to achieve a sense of balance by studying the political circumstances of the Palestinians in Jordan, where most of them lived, in the years 1949–67. An inquiry into the events of this period is crucial to understanding their present conflicts and dilemmas.

My primary motivation to deal with this subject was the desire to know what happened to the Palestinian issue in the interwar period. Equally, I was motivated by the question of why certain things did not happen. Many people since June 1967 have been bothered by the question: Why not create a Palestinian state in the West Bank? I have preferred to ask: What happened in the West Bank before 1967 which kept this issue in a relatively low profile? Why were Palestinian political aspirations muted for so many years?

After the 1948 war, the Palestinian Arabs dispersed to many countries in the Arab world, but most remained in the West Bank or moved to the East Bank, becoming the majority in the Kingdom of Jordan. They became, as the Palestinian writer Muhammed Abu Shilbaya put it, "the salt . . . the light of culture and progress in science, in knowledge and in toil, in schools, universities, the press, factories, and the green fields that have been created from yellow, arid wilderness."[1] Throughout these years the Palestinians kept alive memories of their past and cultivated their heritage. But what happened to their political activities, to their political leadership on the local and national levels, to the many groups in the West Bank that opposed the Jordanian regime, including the supporters of Hajj Amin al-Husseini, the former Mufti of Jerusalem, the Communists, the Ba'thists, the Qawmiyyun al-'arab (Arab Nationalists), and the Tahrir (Liberation) party? Why did these political groups, with their intellectual capacity, social superiority, and political experience with the Jewish community through the Mandate period, not succeed in becoming, in a country where they were the majority, a key political element? Their basic national interests were contradictory to those of King 'Abdallah and his successors, and after the middle of the 1950s they found political alliances as well as financial supporters in Cairo, Damascus, and Baghdad who encouraged them to overthrow the Jordanian regime. However, the Palestinian elite never posed any durable threat to Amman between 1949 and 1967.

Several factors, of course, come immediately to mind: Jordanian military and economic control on the West Bank, Israeli declarations that any change in the political status quo there would be considered a *casus belli,* and the clear interest of Britain and United States in maintaining the status quo. However important the role that external political powers played in West Bank politics, I believe that much of the failure of the Palestinians to realize their political goals for nearly two decades had its roots in their historical record, political values, and social structure. As Palestinians, they were hindered by the 1948 war from establishing independent political authority. As Jordanians, they were dependent on resources allocated by the government. And as Arabs, they relied heavily on pan-Arab and pan-Islamic symbols. "Palestinian in face"—as Yasir 'Arafat put it—"but Arab in heart."[2]

1. See Muhamad Abu Shilbaya, *Al-Tariq ilal-Khalas wal-Huriyya wal-Salam* [The road to redemption, liberation, and peace] (Al-Quds), p. 13, as cited by Yehoshafat Harkabi, "The Palestinians in the Fifties and Their Awakening as Reflected in Their Literature," in *Palestinian Arab Politics* ed. Moshe Ma'oz, (Jerusalem: Jerusalem Academic Press, 1975), p. 61.

2. See *al-Muharrir* (Beirut), November 19, 1968.

What did it mean practically and ideologically to be identified as Palestinians, feel as Arabs, and live as Jordanians? What did it mean to the Jordanian government? How did Amman and the Palestinians handle the problem all these years? What kind of political relations developed? What has been done on both sides of the river? In probing these fundamental questions, I fulfill the dual purpose of providing previously unpublished information about Palestinian and Jordanian politics and of developing certain political concepts that have relevance beyond the situation in the Middle East.

It would have been very difficult for me to explore these questions without the opportunity to use materials in one of the Jordanian archives which covered political events in the West Bank from the mid-1950s to mid-1960s. This archive became available to the Israel State Archives (ISA) after the Six-Day War. I want to thank David Farchi and Shlomo Gazit in Israel's Defense Force for their permission and Dr. Paul A. Alsberg and his staff for their patience and help. I owe a great debt to Amnon Cohen of the Department of History of Muslim Countries at the Institute of Asian and African Studies, the Hebrew University of Jerusalem, and Moshe Ma'oz, the academic director of the Harry S. Truman Institute, who let me use several unpublished papers written under their auspices.

Without Dan Horowitz and Jacob M. Landau, my supervisors in the Department of Political Science of Hebrew University, I would probably be digging in other fields. Without David Apter, Peter Cleaves, William Foltz, Stanley Greenburg, Joseph LaPalombara, Michael Reich, Michael Reisman and James C. Scott—all at Yale University—and Yitzchak Bernstein at Edinburgh University, this book would be completely different; less coherent, more complicated. A fellowship from the Lady Davis Trust made it possible, and Marian Ash at Yale Press with her patience and consistency made it more readable.

1

The Palestinian Arab Community in Jordan

THE ANNEXATION AND ITS CONSEQUENCES

In February 1971, Qadri Tuqan, a Palestinian Arab from Nablus in
the West Bank, who served as a minister in the Jordan government
during the 1960s, died while on a visit to Beirut. His body was re-
turned to Nablus through the East Bank of Jordan. There, his
coffin was wrapped with a Jordanian flag. But when it crossed the
river into the West Bank, a Palestinian flag replaced the Jordanian
one.[1]

Throughout his political life Tuqan, like many other Palestinian
Arabs, had worked for coexistence between Palestinians and Jordanians as a step toward cooperation that might lead to unity with
other Arab countries and to the liberation of Palestine. Yet even in
death, he was unable to escape the tension between his allegiance
to Jordan and his commitment to the Palestinian collective ideal.
What were the origins of this tension? What was its impact on the
political allegiance and political behavior of the Palestinian Arabs?

From May 1948 to the end of the Arab-Israeli War, hundreds of
thousands of Palestinian Arabs moved to the West Bank of the
Jordan River, which had come under the control of the Arab Legion
(Transjordan's and later Jordan's army). Transjordan's military
expansion onto the West Bank after the war was followed in April
1950 by formal annexation. The "Emirate of Transjordan" became
the "Hashemite Kingdom of Jordan."[2] While Israel became a state

---

1. *Le Monde,* March 2, 1971; Malcolm H. Kerr, *The Arab Cold War,* 3rd
ed. (New York: Oxford University Press, 1971), p. 151.

2. On March 1, 1950, a royal decree by King 'Abdallah of Jordan forbade
the use of the word "Palestine" in official documents. The Jordanian govern-

with a Jewish majority, Jordan became a dual society with two main political communities: Palestinian Arab and Transjordanian. This situation set the background for conflict, tension, and allegiance for the next two decades. It is here one must look to determine why Palestinian desires for a "homeland" did not become the major political issue in the Middle East until the late 1960s.

The inclusion of the West Bank in the Kingdom of Jordan created a far-reaching territorial change in the United Nations partition plan of 1947, which divided Palestine into a Jewish state and an Arab state. As a result of the rejection of the partition plan by the Arab states and the Palestinian Arabs, and the outbreak of the 1948 war, most of the territory of the projected Arab state was split between Israel and Jordan. Approximately 2500 square miles were added to the 5600 square miles initially allotted to Israel under the partition plan, and 2200 square miles were annexed by Jordan.[3]

The Jordanian annexation tripled the population under its rule. In 1948, Transjordan's population was 400,000; the annexation added 900,000 Palestinians, half of whom were already inhabitants of the West Bank, while the rest were refugees who fled to both the West Bank and the East Bank from the areas in Palestine that became part of Israel.[4] About 30 percent of the refugees settled in refugee camps, 32 percent in villages, and 38 percent in cities.[5]

ment and newspapers adopted the terms "West Bank" and "East Bank," rather than Palestine and Transjordan, to stress symbolically that the area was now a single state.

3. As a result of the war, Egypt held the 135 square miles of Gaza strip which had been under the British Mandate. See Nadav Safran, *From War to War* (New York: Pegasus, 1969), p. 33.

4. In 1950, the United Nations Economic Mission to the Middle East gave the number of Palestinian refugees as 100,905 in the East Bank and 431,500 in the West Bank. The United Nations Relief and Works Agency (UNRWA) estimated the total number of refugees in both banks in August 31, 1950, as 485,000. See United Nations, General Assembly, *Assistance to Palestine Refugees: Interim Report of the Director of the United Nations Relief and Works Agency for Palestine Refugees in the Near East,* Office Records: Fifth Session, Suppl. 19 (A/1451/Rev. 1), 1951, p. 4; Aqil Abidi, *Jordan: A Political Study, 1948–1957* (New York: Asia Publishing House, 1965), p. 63.

5. See Raphael Patai, ed., *The Hasemite Kingdom of Jordan* (New Haven: Human Relations Area Files, Yale University, 1956), p. 45.

While the population of Jordan was trebled, the area of tilled land increased by only one-third. The flow of refugees raised the population density for tilled land on the East Bank from 80 to 107 and on the West Bank from 200 to 580. As a result of the armistice agreement between Jordan and Israel in April 1949, many villages, especially in the central and northern parts of the West Bank, were particularly hard-hit: their lands, about 144 square miles, were transferred to Israel, leaving some 150,000 people with no land to farm.[6]

Jordan's economy was also disrupted by the annexation settlement. Pressure resulted from the need to find new sources of employment not only for the refugees but also for some of the permanent residents of the West Bank, particularly those whose employment had been closely bound up with areas of Palestine now under Israeli control. In addition, commercial contacts between the West Bank and the rest of the Arab world, carried on primarily by the shipment of goods through Palestine to the sea, were disrupted as a result of the closing of the Jordanian-Israeli border, and goods now had to go through 'Aqaba, Jordan's only port, or by land through Damascus and Beirut.

Jordan's annexation of the West Bank highlighted the socioeconomic differences between the Palestinian and Transjordanian populations. Distinctions were apparent in the degree of urbanization, literacy, health standards, exposure to the mass media, and level of political participation.[7]

The Transjordanians were almost all villagers or nomadic tribesmen, and the urban sector was relatively limited. Of a population of 340,000 in 1943, about half were Bedouin and a third lived in rural areas. Town and city dwellers were a minority, accounting for only about one-fifth of the total.[8] In contrast, about one-third

6. For more details see International Bank for Reconstruction and Development, *The Economic Development of Jordan* (Baltimore: The Johns Hopkins Press, 1957) p. 41; Naseer H. Aruri, *Jordan: A Study in Political Development (1921–1965)* (The Hague: Martinus Nijhoff, 1972), p. 49.

7. On these sociodemographic measures as indicators of the level of modernization of a society see Daniel Lerner, *The Passing of Traditional Society* (New York: Free Press, 1958), pp. 54–65.

8. A. Konikoff, *Transjordan: An Economic Survey,* 2nd ed. (Jerusalem:

of the Arab population of Palestine in 1944 was urban. Most of them were concentrated in twenty-one cities and towns.[9]

The Palestinians' higher rate of urbanization had helped the growth of a relatively extensive labor force, especially in the larger cities like Jerusalem, Jaffa, and Haifa. By the mid-1940s this labor force was over 25,000 strong, and most of it was organized in more than thirty unions operating in the framework of the Federation of Trade Unions and Workers' Organizations established in 1942.[10] No such organized urban labor force had emerged in Transjordan. A rather small step in this direction had been made by Dr. Subhi Abu Ghneima with the Union of Workers of Jordan, but it organized no more than 2000 workers.[11]

There was also a great difference between the East and West Bank populations in terms of educational level. While only about 20 percent of school-age children on the East Bank actually attended school in 1944, 52 percent of Palestinian Arab children did.[12] Differences between the two populations also existed in the area of health. In 1939 there were three physicians for 10,000 Arabs in Palestine; in Transjordan there was only one for 10,000 residents. Moreover, the infant mortality rate among the Palestinian Arab population was 116 per 1000, while among the Transjordanians it was 181 per 1000.[13]

In the realm of communications, in 1944 Transjordan had only one local newspaper, while the Palestinian Arabs had three daily newspapers, ten weeklies, and five quarterlies.[14] Lerner's study of

Economic Research Institute of the Jewish Agency for Palestine, 1946), p. 18.

9. Among these cities were Jerusalem with a population of 60,080 Arabs; Jaffa, 66,280; Haifa, 62,510; Gaza, 34,170; Hebron, 24,560; and Ramallah with 5,080. For more details see Palestine Government, *A Survey of Palestine* (Jerusalem: Government Printer, 1946), pp. 137–39, 148–51; Aruri, *Jordan: Study in Political Development,* p. 35.

10. See C. Issawi, "Labor Relations and Organizations" in *Hashemite Kingdom of Jordan,* ed. Raphael Patai, p. 429.

11. See Walter Z. Laqueur, "Communism in Jordan," *The World Today* 12 (March 1956):109–19.

12. Lerner, *Passing of Traditional Society,* p. 306.

13. Aruri, *Jordan: Study in Political Development,* p. 36.

14. Ibid; Palestine Government, *Survey of Palestine,* p. 717.

the Palestinian and Transjordanian populations in the early 1950s showed that the Palestinians were greater consumers of the mass media than the Transjordanians. This was expresssed, among other ways, by a higher rate of newspaper reading and radio listening.[15]

Apart from the social differences between the two populations, one can point also to a difference in the level of political activity. The struggle in Palestine between the Arab and Jewish communities hastened political development among both groups; the lack of any similar challenge in Transjordan left its population at a lower level of political development.

Recognizing those differences, the Jordanian government restructured the political and administrative organizations it found on the West Bank in order to institutionalize its authority. As a first step the Jordanian government dissolved Palestinian bodies that had been active during the British Mandate in Palestine and during the war. In the earliest period of Transjordanian rule in the West Bank, the military governors forbade local organizations from granting licenses or collecting taxes and transferred these functions to the military command. All functionaries appointed by the Arab Higher Committee, the major political organization of the Palestinian Arabs in Palestine, were ordered to cease their activities, and the population was ordered to obey the instructions only of the military administration. The Arab Higher Committee had been trying to establish an administration of its own before the Arab intervention in the 1948 war, but the measures taken by the Arab Legion Command succeeded in putting a stop to the activity of its "national committees."[16]

The Arab Legion also acted to restrict the activities of the Palestinian irregular forces, "al-Jihad al-Moqaddas," most of whom were concentrated in the Jerusalem area where they trained. During the war, they had carried out their operations from bases behind Legion lines but did little to help the Transjordanian forces hold the

15. Lerner, *Passing of Traditional Society*, pp. 309–10. There was no radio-broadcasting station in Transjordan before 1949. The kingdom's first one was set up in Ramallah during the 1948 war.

16. *Ha'aretz* (Tel-Aviv), May 23, 1948; Yoseph Nevo, "Mediniuyto ha-palestinait shel 'Abdallah 1945–1948 ['Abdallah's Palestinian policy] (M.A. thesis for the Hebrew University of Jerusalem, 1971), p. 69.

front.[17] They were disbanded and disarmed by the Arab Legion to keep them from becoming a focus of power opposed to the political center in Amman.

The next step in unifying the two banks was to establish over-arching and integrative institutions. The Jordanian military adminis-tration, which had operated in the West Bank since its entry, gave way to a civil administration after a short period. A royal decree of March 6, 1949, appointed three civilian governors: Raghib al-Nashashibi for the Jerusalem district, Ahmad Khalil for Ramallah and the northern areas, and Na'im 'Abd al-Hadi for Hebron. A civilian governor-general for the West Bank was also appointed.[18]

The second stage of the official process toward administrative unification was a decree of December 1949 officially subordinating West Bank officials to the government in Amman. The governors of the West Bank were responsible to the minister of the interior for everything except matters controlled by the prime minister and the cabinet. The office of governor-general of the West Bank was to be abolished once the directors of the various departments there were integrated into the Jordanian ministries.[19]

After the 1950 general elections, an attempt was made to integrate the different legal systems of the two banks. The government established a legal commission headed by Ibrahim Hashim, a Pales-tinian originally from Nablus who emigrated to Transjordan in the 1920s. Composed of judges and lawyers from both banks, the com-mission proposed recommendations that provided for compromises between and integration of the two systems.[20] At the same time

17. See John Bagot Glubb, *A Soldier with the Arabs* (London: Hedder and Stoughton, 1957), p. 192.

18. See *al-Jarida al-Rasmiyya* [The official gazette], April 4, 1949.

19. Ibid, December 17, 1949.

20. The differences between the legal systems of the two banks were quite clear. While the British Mandate legal system had gradually been introduced in Palestine, Ottoman law was maintained in Transjordan. Awareness of the differences between the two legal systems and of the difficulty in integrating them led to the decision by Amman, made immediately after the Arab Legion took control of the West Bank, that all laws from the Mandate period would remain in force until the promulgation of Jordanian laws. See E. T. Mogan-nam, "Developments in the Legal System of Jordan," *Middle East Journal* 6 (1952):194–206.

the *dinar* was made the sole legal currency in the kingdom from September 1, 1950.[21]

In addition to establishing an overarching and integrative system, Amman extended its authority over the West Bank by setting up new frameworks and projects to respond to the needs of the population. The economic hardships suffered by the West Bankers led to the establishment of a Ministry of Social Welfare in 1951. It was made up of three branches: the Office for the Development of Cooperatives, to help cooperatives with loans; the Social Welfare Office, to provide material assistance to families in need—especially in the villages near the Israeli border; and the Employment Office, to improve working conditions.[22] Local organizations to aid the refugees were created to supplement financial support from the United Nations and the Arab states. Moreover, on August 14, 1949, a Ministry for Refugee Affairs was established by royal decree, and Raghib al-Nashashibi, the former mayor of Jerusalem, was appointed minister.[23] The ministry initiated and encouraged development plans to provide employment and to contribute to the refugees' rehabilitation. One such plan was the so-called Constructive Scheme near Jericho which was initiated by the Palestinian politician Musa al-'Alami. On July 22, 1949, in order to implement the plan, the government promised to make available 20,000 *dunam* of land in the Jordan Valley and allocated £10,000 to pay for land reclamation.[24] All of these activities reflected Amman's attempts to extend its authority over the population in the new territories.

The appointment of members of the West Bank elite to senior posts in the government was another way to reach this goal. Opening the door to incorporating the Palestinian elite in the existing polit-

---

It is worthwhile noting the similar decision by Israel, which also adopted Mandate government law, except for laws stemming from the 1939 British White Paper.

21. *Al-Difa'*, September 13, 1950.

22. *Dalil al-Urdun al-sihafi* [Guide to the Jordanian press] (Amman, 1959), p. 51; Abidi, *Jordan: Political Study*, p. 171.

23. *Hamizrah Hehadash* [The New East] 1 (1949):64. Hereafter cited as *HMH*.

24. *Al-Difa'*, June 24, 1949. For details on the development of the scheme on the Musa al-'Alami farm near Jericho see G. Furlonge, *Palestine Is My Country: The Story of Musa Alami* (New York: Praeger, 1969) pp. 167–211.

ical institutions required doubling the membership of the legislature from 20 to 40, with each bank having 20 seats. Senate membership was also doubled, from 10 to 20 delegates, with parity between the banks.[25] King 'Abdallah also appointed West Bank residents to senior executive offices, and the services and ranges of subjects they dealt with were broadened. Three West Bank Arabs, for instance, served as ministers in the Jordanian cabinet in 1949: Ruhi 'Abd al-Hadi, from Nablus, in foreign affairs; Khlusi Khayri, from Ramallah, in trade and agriculture; and Musa Nasir, also from Ramallah, in communication.[26]

After annexation, the central authorities in Amman tended to place Palestinians from the West Bank in senior offices and administrative posts that were directly related to West Bank problems. Palestinians were appointed provincial governors as well as given positions on the Israeli-Jordanian Mixed Armistice Commission, in the representation of refugee affairs, and in the economic, educational, and judicial sectors.[27] Palestinians also held senior administrative positions in the ministries of Agriculture, Economics, Education, Development, and Foreign Affairs.

Jordan's annexation of the West Bank therefore required the establishment of new roles and restructured political frameworks, as well as a policy of selective appointment of Palestinians to political positions, to ensure the bonds of the West Bank to Amman. East Bank loyalists, some of whom were Palestinians who had emigrated to Transjordan in the 1920s and 1930s, and cooperative leaders on the West Bank gained high positions in the new political system. The latter, however, did not hold the most powerful positions in the cabinet: the prime ministership, the deputy prime ministership, the minister of the interior, and later the minister of information.[28] Whatever the direct impact of Jordan's annexation

25. See *HMH* 1 (1950):302–03. For a list of the members of the first Senate see also Zvi Ne'eman, *Mamlekhet 'Abdallah leahar ha-sipuah* ['Abdallah's kingdom after the annexation] (Jerusalem: Israel Foreign Ministry, 1950), pp. 71–72.

26. See Abidi, *Jordan: Political Study,* p. 65.

27. *HMH* 1 (1949):60.

28. Uriel Dann, "Regime and Opposition in Jordan since 1949" in *Society and Political Structure in the Arab World* ed. Menachem Milson (New York: Humanities Press, 1973), p. 150.

was on the political life of specific Palestinian leaders, it had a broad effect on the extent and type of relations that were developed between Amman and the West Bank.

PALESTINIAN PRIMORDIALISM AND JORDANIAN CIVIL ORDER

Amman's efforts to unify its enlarged territory and the unstable political and economic conditions in the West Bank after annexation led various Palestinian groups to emigrate from the West to the East Bank. The shift in population made the East Bank more heterogeneous, inhabited by both Jordanians and Palestinians, while the West Bank remained homogeneous, inhabited only by Palestinians.

The social homogeneity of the West Bank helped the Palestinian community there preserve its primordial attachment[29] to Palestine despite the radical change in its political status from an autonomous community with interstate relations with Amman to a fragmented society with intrastate relations with Amman. Palestinian primordialism had its roots in the dominant role that local institutions like the family, the clan, the village, and the city played in people's lives. Especially in the rural areas of Palestine during Ottoman rule and the British Mandate, these institutions and their political activity were stronger among the inhabitants of the western areas (the West Bank) than in the coastal plain and Galilee areas from which the Palestinian refugees came. "The reason for this difference," as Yehoshua Porath explained, "lay in social variance between these regions. In the Judean mountains and Samaria [the West Bank] there was a continuity of settlement from previous ages. The villages

29. "A primordial attachment," according to Geertz, "relates to the 'given' or more precisely . . . the assumed 'givens'—of social existence: immediate contiguity and kin connection mainly but beyond them the givenness that stems from being born into a particular religious community, speaking a particular language, or even a dialect of a language, and following particular social practices. These congruities of blood, speech, custom and so on, are seen to have an ineffable, and at times overpowering, coerciveness in and of themselves. . . . in modernizing societies where the tradition of civil politics is weak . . . primordial attachments tend . . . to be repeatedly, in some cases almost continually, proposed and widely acclaimed as preferred bases for the demarcation of autonomous political units." Clifford Geertz, *The Interpretation of Cultures,* (New York: Basic Books, 1973), pp. 259–60.

were organized in subdistricts, at the head of which were the local sheikhs. . . . On the other hand, the villages in the coastal plain and in the valleys had been set up in later periods, after the terror of the Bedouins had largely passed and after the latter had themselves begun to settle down in the empty regions of the country. In these villages no social-administrative units had yet crystallized, nor did they have their own leadership."[30]

During the almost thirty years of the British Mandate in Palestine (1920–48) Palestinian primordialism was strengthened as the Palestinian Arabs became politically aware, largely in response to British policy and to Jewish activity. Both of these were considered by the Palestinian Arab ideology and by many Palestinian political groups as a threat to the Arab majority in Palestine and as such to the very existence of the Arab community there. "We cannot patiently watch our homeland pass into others' hands," protested Palestinian Arabs in Ramleh and Lydda. "Either us or the Zionist! There is no room for both elements struggling together in the same area. The laws of nature require that one side be defeated. We want life and they are striving for it, but life is indivisible. There is no escaping the fact that one of us must win."[31]

The new political circumstances at the end of the 1948 war created three societies living in two states—with the Palestinian Arab society living on both sides of the line. This state of affairs can be illustrated as in the accompanying diagram.[32] The fears of the Palestinians became reality. The dispartiy between the social and political boundaries of the Palestinian community increased the efforts of the Palestinian Arabs inside and outside the West Bank to regain Palestine within the British Mandatory boundaries. Palestinian primordialism revolved around interstate territorial attachments which involved Israeli land as well as the West Bank. Their desires provided a focus for a potential conflict between the Palestinians and Israel on the one hand and between the Palestinians and the Jordanian regime on the other hand.

30. Yehoshua Porath, *The Emergence of the Palestinian-Arab National Movement 1918–1929* (London: Frank Cass, 1974), p. 287.

31. Ibid, p. 50.

32. My thanks to Dr. Erik Cohen of the Department of Sociology of the Hebrew University, who drew my attention to this visual illustration of the state of affairs.

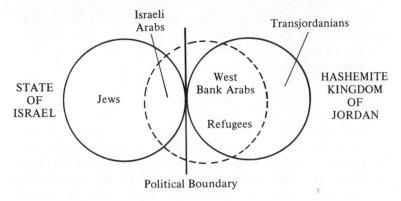

During the 1948 war and in the first years after the annexation, there had always been people within the Palestinian leadership who challenged Jordan's activities on the West Bank and who sought to realize Palestinian allegiance through Palestinian, pan-Arab, or pan-Islam options. In September 1949, for instance, Palestinian leaders established, under the auspices of the Arab League, the ill-fated all-Palestine government (Hukumat 'Umum Filastin) in the Gaza strip designed to regain Palestine within the Mandatory boundaries.[33] From 1954 on, political groupings in the West Bank, like al-Ba'th and the National Socialists, tended to express their Palestinian allegiance in the pan-Arab option, which was associated with the Nasir regime, although some saw it embodied in the Damascus Ba'thist regime. Others, like the Muslim Brotherhood and the Tahrir (Liberation) party, sought to fulfill their political desires in Palestine through activity in pan-Islam movements. Behind the activity of all these groups lay their primordial attachment to Palestine, which, as we have seen, ran across the existing boundaries of Jordan. Inevitably, Palestinian primordialism created a feeling of ambivalence among the Palestinians about their political allegiance to the regime in Amman.

33. On the formation of the all-Palestine government see 'Arif al-'Arif, *Al-Nakba, nakbat bait al-maqdis wa-al-firdaws al-mafqud: 1947-1955* [The disaster, the calamity of the Holy Land and the loss of Paradise: 1947-1955] (Beirut: al-Maktaba al-'asriyya lil tiba'a wa-al-Nashr, undated), pp. 89, 703–05; Abidi, *Jordan: Political Study*, pp. 49–52.

One can point to Palestinian leaders in the West Bank, especially those who belonged to the Nashashibi faction, who supported King 'Abdallah's political goal of incorporating Palestinian territories into his kingdom. Nevertheless, many of them tended to make their support conditional on his willingness eventually to include all of Palestine in his kingdom and on the termination of the political independence of the Jewish community there. This attitude was most strikingly articulated by the Jerusalem and Ramallah delegates to the Palestinian Congress, also known as the Jericho Conference, which was arranged by King 'Abdallah and his Palestinian supporters on December 1, 1948, to endow with legitimacy his annexation of Palestinian territories to Jordan. Only a few, however, like Sheikh Muhammad 'Ali al-Ja'bari of Hebron and Wadi' Da'mas of Beit Jalla, wanted to give 'Abdallah a free hand in solving the Palestine problem.[34] The attitudes of the Jerusalem and Ramallah delegates were reflected in some of the decisions of the Jericho Conference. It was resolved, for example, that "the Conference sees Palestine as a single indivisible unit. Any solution incompatible with this situation will not be considered final. . . . The Conference recognizes His Majesty King 'Abdallah as King of all Palestine and greets him and his gallant army as well as the Arab armies that fought and are still fighting in defense of Palestine."[35]

One can conclude that, despite internal conflict over a broad range of issues, Palestinian leaders inside as well as outside the West Bank strongly agreed on the need to preserve the Arab character of Palestine. Consequently, they were unanimous in their desire for some Arab political authority that would include the entire territory of Palestine within the British Mandate's boundaries, though the exact form and operation of this authority was a subject of controversy among the various political streams.

In this respect, for the king's Palestinian opponents and many of his supporters, the conflict between the Arab and Jewish communities over Palestine was a fundamental issue that involved a total

34. 'Aziz Shihadah, "Megamot he-haqiqa ha-yardenit ba-Gada ha-Ma'aravit" [The purposes of Jordanian legislation in the West Bank], *HMH* 20 (1970): 166.

35. 'Arif al-'Arif, *Al-Nakba*, pp. 877–78.

opposition of interests. But 'Abdallah, who sought cooperation with the Jewish community in Palestine and later with Israel in order to strengthen his political position in the West Bank, preferred to see the conflict as a problem to be handled by processes of political bargaining, with due regard for the balance of power in the region.[36] This conflicting interpretation was mostly a result of the contradiction between 'Abdallah's political goals in Palestine and those of the Palestinians during the Mandate period—a contradiction that stemmed from 'Abdallah's desire to prevent the creation of an independent Palestinian political existence in Palestine, which was perceived by him as a potential rival.[37] Opposing evaluations of the outcome of the 1948 war reflected this contradiction. From the standpoint of the Palestinian Arabs, the 1948 war had ended in utter defeat. For King 'Abdallah, however, the war had enhanced his political authority and increased his military power.

These opposing viewpoints critically affected the way each side defined its objectives in the conflict with Israel. King 'Abdallah tended to treat the Arab-Israeli issue as a residual border conflict. The Palestinians, on the other hand, considered it a clash of destinies that needed a radical solution.[38] In this respect, Amman defined its political objectives in terms of the actual needs of the existing Jordanian civil order, while the West Bank population defined its political objectives in terms of the realization of the national ambitions of the Arab people of Palestine.

36. On the Israeli-Jordanian discussion in late 1948 and the beginning of 1949 over the possibility of political settlement see, for example, 'Abdallah al-Tall, *Zikhronot 'Abdallah al-Tall* [The memoirs of 'Abdallah al-Tall] (Tel-Aviv: Ma'arokhot, 1964), pp. 303–26; and also Ben Gurion's interview with the Kimche brothers, in the Hebrew edition: "The negotiations reached an advanced stage. Israel agreed to grant Jordan a free port—at Haifa or Jaffa—and a corridor to it. The parties were discussing the width of the corridor when King 'Abdallah was shot and killed [in July 1951]. . . . If 'Abdallah had not been murdered a full peace would have been signed between Israel and the Kingdom of Jordan." Jon and David Kimche, *Mishnei evrei ha-giv'ah* [Both sides of the hill], 2nd ed. (Tel-Aviv: Ma'arakhot, 1973), p. 263.

37. For details on 'Abdallah's attitude toward the Palestinians, see Yoseph Nevo, *"Mediniuyto ha-palestinait shel 'Abdallah,"* pp. 1–14, 27–46.

38. On this distinction see Nadav Safran, *From War to War*, p. 22.

The political differences between Amman and the West Bank, however, were not apparent in their attitudes toward political change. Both sides considered political change necessary. Indeed, in the first few years after annexation 'Abdallah was in contact with Syrian and Lebanese leaders about some sort of political union that would embrace Jordan, Syria, and Lebanon and would realize his political dream of a "Greater Syria."[39] Later on, this led to the attempt by King Hussein, who came to power in 1953, to join the Baghdad Pact and to the federation with Iraq proclaimed on February 14, 1958. Both Amman and the political groupings in the West Bank were dissatisfied with the political situation that developed after the 1948 war. Each side drew different conclusions, however, about the gap between their goals. Amman wanted to alter its relations with some of the Arab states in order to reinforce its position in the West Bank while simultaneously maintaining the status quo on its western, that is, Israeli, border. The West Bank political circles, on the other hand, wished to change the relations between themselves and Amman as well as between Amman and the other Arab states in order to change the status quo on the kingdom's western border.

Under these circumstances one might have expected tension between Palestinian primordialism and the requirements of Jordanian civil order to strengthen separatist currents among the Palestinian community and to lead to a Palestinian appeal for an autonomous existence and an inevitable clash between the two political communities. In reality, however, the tension between them was balanced to some extent by the ideal of Arab unity, which was shared by both Palestinians and Jordanians and which served as an ideological moderator between them. According to the pan-Arab

39. On the correspondence between 'Abdallah and the British government on this matter before the 1948 war, see *al-Kitab al-urduni al-abyad* (the Jordanian White Paper) (Amman, 1947), pp. 19–23. On 'Abdallah's repeated attempts to achieve his ends in the 1950s, including his contacts with the Syrian and Lebanese governments see his memoirs, *al-Takmila min mudhak-karat Sahib al-Jalala al-Hashimiyya al-Malik 'Abdallah ibn Hussayn* [A supplement to His Hashemite Excellency King 'Abdallah Ibn Hussein's memoirs] (Amman, 1951), pp. 307–08, and the diary of the former foreign minister of Lebanon, Riyad al-Sulh, in *al-Hayat* (Beirut), August 30, 1953.

view, the secession of the West Bank from Jordan was undesirable, since it meant further fragmenting the Arab world. Yet even those who did not subscribe to this pan-Arab belief accepted the argument that, politically, redemption of Palestine could be fulfilled only through Arab unity. The conflict between the goals of Palestinian primordialism and Jordanian civil order was balanced therefore not only by the Palestinian fear of Israeli occupation in case of secession from Jordan but also by an ideological argument derived from their pan-Arab attachment and embodied in the idea of Arab unity.

This Palestinian attitude toward Amman was reflected a few months after annexation in a series of articles by Qadri Tuqan, at that time a young Palestinian critic from Nablus. As he put it, "Jordan, on both banks . . . has a special character compatible with its annexation to every other Arab state. The Jordanian feels the danger that threatens Arab existence in all the countries more than any other Arab. Moreover, there is no 'local patriotism' or 'regional pride' in this state, but a willingness and ability to integrate rapidly with a broader sector."[40] The regime in Amman encouraged this attitude among the Palestinians. Its activities, according to its own public statements, were guided by the same political orientations and ultimate objectives as those current in the West Bank.

The inferior geopolitical position of the West Bank compared to the East Bank also played a balancing role by weakening the potential radical influence of Palestinian primordialism on relations between the banks. It is true that the Palestinians, before and during the Mandate period, had reached a higher level of modernization and social and political development than the Transjordanians. However, the sense of geopolitical insecurity on the part of West Bank residents was magnified by their loss of the war and by their being surrounded on one side by a hostile and threatening Israel and on the other by a suspicious regime in Amman. The weak geopolitical position of the Palestinians was further aggravated by Amman's monopoly of both military power and foreign economic aid, which increased the West Bank's dependence on Amman.

40. Qadri Tuqan, *Filastin*, December 8, 1951. In the concluding article of the series he explains: "The golden path leads to union with another Arab country. The government, the legislature, and the enlightened stratum must realize this and consider deeply." See *Filastin*, December 15, 1951.

The West Bank Arabs' attachment to the ideal of Arab unity and awareness of their geopolitical inferiority provided the basis for exchanges with the regime in Amman. The Palestinians supplied resources of skilled manpower to fill vital economic, administrative, and public service functions. In return, Amman allowed them some opportunities for action and some freedom to maneuver in both the political and economic spheres. This interdependence of the parties increased as Jordanian rule persisted in the West Bank. The possibility of a one-sided dependence of the Palestinians on Amman or vice versa was ruled out.

While interdependence reduced conflict between the West Bank and Amman, it did not eliminate tension. Despite the balancing influences of the ideal of Arab unity and the West Bank's geopolitical inferiority, Palestinian primordialism continued to obstruct efforts by the Jordanian authorities to acquire full legitimacy in the West Bank. The political and social differences between the two banks exacerbated the struggle between the ruling elite in Amman and elite circles in the West Bank over the allocation of resources and rewards and even over the rules of exchange themselves. As the struggle continued, the Palestinians were willing to accept Jordanian rule as long as they could play a part in the definition of political goals and in the allocation of resources.

Both sides thus came to a realistic assessment of their relationship in which political goals were guided by a consideration of real power relations in addition to ultimate objectives. The incongruence of the aims of the parties grew increasingly evident not because of differences over matters of principle but because of differences over intermediate-range political objectives of practical significance. Each side tried to develop optimum patterns of action to serve its objectives. Amman set out to establish roles and institutions that would incorporate the West Bank into the kingdom, while the Palestinian opposition concentrated on presenting various demands to the Jordanian administration.

One should note, however, that political organizations opposing the Jordanian regime—like al-Ba'th, the Communists, al-Qawmiyyun al-'arab, or al-Tahrir—were active not only among the Palestinians on the West Bank but also among the Jordanians on the East Bank. Similarly, supporters of the regime were found not only among

Bedouins and the military establishment of the East Bank but also in Palestinian commercial and political circles on both banks. In this respect, "Amman" and "the West Bank" cannot be taken literally to represent the Jordanian regime and its opposition. Nevertheless, most of the opposition groups and "the majority of their leaders and members throughout Jordan"—as Amnon Cohen, a student of the political parties in the West Bank, put it—"and generally the most prominent, were from the West Bank. . . . Their numerical strength makes it possible to view . . . [them] as primarily belonging to the West Bank."[41] This political difference between the two banks allows one to distinguish between the Palestinian and Jordanian sides without fear of misleading.

During most of the period 1949–67 political groups on both sides tended to opt for solutions that balanced conflicting pressures and cooperative interests rather than risk one-sided solutions. Coexistence between them relied, for the most part, on flexible arrangements. The government in Amman initiated these arrangements, but flexibility was also encouraged by the tendency of Palestinian political groups to cope with tension with Amman by separating Jordanian "official" identity from Palestinian and pan-Arab allegiance. The former was embodied in their citizenship in the Kingdom of Jordan, while the latter was reflected in their allegiance to Arab regimes such as those in Cairo and Damascus. In sum, the political behavior of both sides encouraged the emergence of relatively durable patterns despite the fact that, stemming from unresolved conflict as they did, they were inherently transitory.

How did these political arrangements work to bridge the gap between Palestinian desires and Jordanian interests? What was the political reality they had to face?

In the next four chapters I examine these questions from the standpoint of legitimacy, identity, and power relations in the years 1949–67. In the last chapter I discuss the conditions that maintained the coexistence of the two banks despite the prolonged conflict between them.

41. See Amnon Cohen, "Political Parties in the West Bank under the Hashemite Regime," in *Palestinian Arab Politics*, ed. Moshe Ma'oz (Jerusalem: Jerusalem Academic Press, 1975), p. 48.

2

Legitimacy and Crisis
(1949–1954 and 1957–1961)

THE PROBLEM OF CONDITIONAL LEGITIMACY

In the election campaign of 1962 for the Jordanian Parliament, one of the Jerusalem candidates appealed to his audience to consider the relationship with Jordan: "I would like you to turn and look at the palaces which have been built in Amman and not in Jerusalem. They were built after 1948 on the shoulders of Palestine."[1] After fourteen years of Jordanian rule in the West Bank, the main issue for Palestinians was still the belief that Amman preferred the East Bank.

The long-term conflict between Palestinians and Jordan made it hard for Palestinians to offer loyalty to Amman. But there were few options. They could not challenge the regime's political goals because they lacked the material resources needed to fight for political revision. They were left in a difficult position, which increased their willingness to cooperate politically as well as economically with Jordan.

Politically, radical activities to separate the West Bank from Jordan seem to have come to a halt within the Palestinian community a short time after the annexation. Only a small element, mostly Communists and the supporters of the former Palestinian Mufti, Hajj Amin al-Husseini, strongly rejected the legitimacy of rule by Amman in the years 1949–51. Except for this short period

---

1. See Archives of Jordanian Security Services, in Israel State Archives, Jerusalem, File 406–9 (hereafter cited as ISA); Eliezer Be'eri, "Ma'amada shel Yerushalayim" [The status of Jerusalem], mimeographed (n.p., n.d.), p. 9.

of separatist activity, there was no strong separatist current in the West Bank that posed a threat to the Jordanian regime until the re-emergence of the slogan "Palestinian entity" in the period 1959–62.

The separatism that did exist had been strongest among the Mufti's supporters in the Hebron district, which had been under Egyptian control for a few months during the 1948 war. In 1949 there were rumors of attempts to have inhabitants of the region sign a petition for the establishment of a Palestinian government. There were also rumors that the former Mufti intended to travel to Washington for a meeting with President Harry Truman in order to persuade him to support the 1947 United Nations partition plan in return for which the Mufti would sign treaties of friendship with the United States and Israel.[2]

There were isolated expressions of separatist attitudes by Hajj Amin's supporters from time to time in later periods. In early November 1957, for instance, the Jordanian commander of the Jenin district in the West Bank reported rumors spread by Hajj Amin supporters about a meeting between the Hajj and President Nasir in which the latter is supposed to have stated that he favored the expulsion of Jordan from the West Bank and the appointment of the former Mufti as "Governor of Palestine."[3] These themes faded quite quickly, however, and did not reemerge until 1959.

The Communists, who from the Mandate period until June 1951 continued to use the name "League for National Liberation," expounded the clearest and most consistent separatist line in the first years after annexation. Their attitude was determined by their support of the United Nations partition plan and by their opposi-tion to Jordanian activity in the West Bank. In the first years after annexation the Communists still hoped that the partition plan could be put into effect and that "alongside the State of Israel there would arise a Palestinian Arab state on the West Bank of the Jordan, linked, somehow or other, to Israel . . . separate from the British-dominated Hashemite kingdom."[4]

2. See ISA, File 928–6; Eliezer Be'eri, "Megamot seperatistiyot" [Separa-tist tendencies], mimeographed (n.p., n.d.), p. 3.
3. ISA, File 631–26.
4. Be'eri, "Megamot seperatistiyot," p. 7.

In 1951, there was a shift in the Communist position on relations between the two banks; gradually separatism gave way to a call for "the solidarity of the Palestinian and Jordanian peoples." Moreover, a statement issued by the Central Committee of the League for National Liberation on June 26, 1951, called for Palestinian participation in the elections to the House of Representatives set for August 29, 1951.[5]

This change in the Communist position was not necessarily related to internal changes in Jordan. The Arab Communist parties had been swinging back and forth between a Marxist internationalist orientation and Arab nationalism since the 1920s. The nationalist currents came to hold the upper hand, and this was reflected in the change in views on separatism in the West Bank, which affected the attitude toward Israel.

Thus, from mid-1951 on, Communist groups on the West Bank tended to resign themselves to the union of the banks. The change of their name from League for National Liberation to Jordanian Communist party in June 1951 also expressed their willingness to see the West Bank as part of the Kingdom of Jordan.[6]

A similar trend is apparent among other opposition parties in the West Bank, such as the Ba'th, al-Qawmiyyun al-'arab (Arab Nationalists), and the Tahrir (Liberation) party. Despite their expressed goal of bringing about a change in the Jordanian regime, they found ideological justification for their neglect of the separatist cause during most of the period of Jordanian rule in the West Bank. According to Eliezer Be'eri, "Palestinian personalities and groups, which wanted to change interstate relations in the Arab world, did not want to establish yet another border, but to wipe away the existing ones. . . . One of the arguments against the Hashemites was the accusation that they had introduced a split among Arabs, and, clearly, no separatist conclusions were drawn from this attitude."[7]

The close economic relations that developed between the West

5. Ibid., p. 10.

6. See Amnon Cohen, "The Jordanian Communist Party in the West Bank, 1950–1960," in *The USSR and the Middle East*, ed. Michael Confino and Shimon Shamir (New York: John Wiley and Sons, 1973), p. 420.

7. Be'eri, "Megamot seperatistiyot," p. 5.

Bankers and Amman immediately after annexation can also be taken to indicate growing dependence on Jordan and a narrowing of the options open to the Palestinians. Indeed, demands and pressures were directed at the Jordanian government by West Bank landowners, merchants, entrepreneurs, and unemployed to undertake economic activity compatible with the new political situation.

Landowners and farmers demanded government assistance in developing their farms. They asked for low-interest loans like those introduced by the British during the last years of the Mandate in Palestine. The owners of land and orchards left in Israeli territory under the armistice agreement demanded that the Jordanian government facilitate access to their property.[8] They believed that, if the central authorities in Amman were willing, a solution could be found to the problem.

The merchants objected to Jordan's customs policy, which restricted imports because of limited foreign currency reserves. They also claimed that West Bank merchants were discriminated against in the issuance of import licenses—a complaint that seems quite reasonable given that two-thirds of the import licenses were given to East Bank residents.[9] Industrial circles also demanded that the government adopt a protectionist policy for local products on the same terms as those for industrial products made on the East Bank. In early January 1950, the merchants asked that a protective tariff be imposed on competitive imports.[10]

8. On these demands see *Filastin*, August 10, 1949, and January 1, 1950. For more details see Gadi Zilberman, "Temurot kalkaliyot ba-ʿir Shchem ba-shanim, 1949–1967" [Economic change in Nablus in the years 1949–1967] mimeographed (Institute of Asian and African Studies, The Hebrew University of Jerusalem, 1972).

9. An example of the sense of economic deprivation in the West Bank is provided by a letter of protest sent to the government by the West Bank Chamber of Commerce: "The problem of imports is still the most important one faced by the West Bank. There are divisions and discriminations between East and West Bank importers. . . . In the present situation the importers are divided into two groups: East Bank importers and West Bank importers. The former are well treated and favored by the authorities, the latter are not. . . . The West Bank importers and merchants are embittered by the inequalities between the two banks in economic matters." *al-Difaʿ* April 13, 1950; "Temurot kalkaliyot," p. 4.

10. *Filastin*, January 27, 1950.

The character of political and economic activity by West Bank Arabs during the first years of Jordanian rule thus indicates that, despite the basic political contradiction between the two banks, there was some tendency toward partial cooperation on economic affairs. West Bank political circles were faced with a dilemma: in order to challenge Amman's policy they needed the material resources that only an effective political center, such as the one in Amman, could supply. At the same time, accepting support and assistance from this center could be interpreted as willingness to acquiesce, implicitly or explicitly, in Amman's policy.

This ambivalence among the Palestinians toward Jordanian rule in the West Bank provided the foundation for relations based on Palestinian willingness to accept Jordan's authority in the West Bank as long as it did not contradict Palestinian interests. In other words: the Palestinians were willing to grant conditional legitimacy to the Jordanian regime in the West Bank. The pattern of conditional legitimacy relied less on the similarities or differences between the ultimate goals of Amman and of the Palestinians than on the concrete meaning of these goals; it served therefore as a compromising element between Palestinian desires and Jordanian interests. From the Palestinian standpoint, conditional legitimacy did not prevent them from expressing their ambivalent attitude toward Amman. At the same time, it permitted them to avoid committing themselves to clear-cut decisions on their goals, which might have resulted in a clash with Amman. From Amman's point of view, the pattern of conditional legitimacy, although it did not offer free rein in the West Bank, at least provided a way for the regime to strengthen its authority through manipulative activities rather than confrontation.

The pattern of conditional legitimacy depended on the willingness of Amman and the West Bank to handle their conflict through a process of political bargaining. The pattern gained strength as long as it demonstrated a capacity to serve the interests of both sides. However, the more able one party became in advancing its political goals the more difficult it was to handle the conflict through a bargaining process, and the pattern of conditional legitimacy tended to weaken. Then, as the probability of success of independent action decreased, the likelihood increased of handling the conflict through a bargaining process.

I now want to examine the relations between Amman and the West Bank in situations where the pattern of conditional legitimacy was weak. I focus on the causes that brought about the weakness of and the crisis in conditional legitimacy as reflected in the large gap between the political objectives of Amman and the West Bank and in the weakness of the bargaining process. During the first period, 1949–54, the radical Arab regimes had still not made their influence felt to any great extent on the political behavior of the West Bank. In the second period, 1957–61, the influence of the Arab regimes on the behavior of the Palestinian political groupings increased. The years 1955–57 and 1961–67 saw the pattern of conditional legitimacy grow stronger.

THE WEAKNESS OF THE CONDITIONAL
LEGITIMACY PATTERN

Issues in Conflict

In the years 1949–54 the Amman regime was confident that it could handle conflict with the West Bank without any meaningful compromise toward the political opposition there. Its confidence derived from the fact that during this period there were no Arab regimes to which the Palestinian opposition could turn for support. The gap between the objectives of Amman and the Palestinians was reflected in the negative attitude of the West Bank opposition toward Amman's policy on a number of foreign as well as domestic issues.

Israel

The opposition of political parties in the West Bank to Amman's policy toward Israel centered on the political contacts between Israel and Jordan. The administration was, for example, sharply criticized for signing the General Armistice Agreement at Rhodes, which involved the transfer of 144 square miles of territory to Israel and left 150,000 people landless. The Ba'thist leader from Ramallah, 'Abdallah al-Rimawi, reacted strongly to the land transfer in the following comment on Jordan's action: "I see heads," he cried, "that are already ripe, and the time has come to cut them off."[11] He accused Jordan and other Arab governments of conspiring with Britain and the United States from the "Palestine disaster" right up to the signing of the armistice agreement with Israel.[12] The issue was also raised by opposition members of Parliament from the West Bank like 'Abdallah Na'was and Anwar al-Khatib from Jerusalem, Rashad Maswada, Sa'id 'Abd al-Fatah al-'Izza, Yusuf 'Abbas 'Umri from Hebron, and Hafiz Hamdallah and Hashim Jayusi from Tulkarm. "Whereas from time to time," they argued in a memorandum to the government, "some of the territory of the state has been yielded on the pretext of a border rectification . . . and with regard to the rumors and suppositions involved . . . we consider it necessary that the House of Representatives examine the information and documents held by the government concerning the Rhodes Agreement and everything related to it, such as conversations, agreements, changes of maps and borders. . . . It is absolutely impossible that such things be done without the knowledge of this House, particularly when they concern the disaster which struck the country as a whole and the inhabitants of the forward areas in particular."[13]

Most of the criticism, however, concerned King 'Abdallah's attempts to reach a peace agreement with Israel. The position the king adopted indicated that he did not in principle regard the territorial and refugee problems as non-negotiable. Negotiations were

11. This statement was originally an antirevolutionary one, attributed to Hajjaj bin Yusuf, governor of Iraq, and was directed against his domestic opponents. Here the phrase is used by the opposition to describe the regime.

12. See al-Ba'th, April 20, 1951.

13. Al-Difa', January 14, 1953. In the debate that followed, Hashim Jayusi voiced strong criticism of the government: "I was not silent about the crime . . . while it was being committed; I did not let it pass in silence when I was a minister in the government, and I shall not let it pass in silence as long as I live. . . . There are hundreds of thousands of citizens who were burnt by the fire that robbed them of their livings, which were given to the Jews without a fight after they [the citizens] had defended them with their blood and soul." See al-Difa', January 27, 1953.

conducted intermittently in the years 1948 and 1949 in meetings between Israeli and Jordanian representatives in London, Paris, and the king's palace at Shuna. The former Jordanian military governor of Jerusalem, 'Abdallah al-Tall, who took part in the negotiations, wrote in his memoirs that the king tried in these talks to get the Israelis to cede Lydda, Ramleh, and the Arab suburbs in the Israeli part of Jerusalem and to let their Palestinian inhabitants return.[14] However, when al-Tall leaked word of the talks in July 1949, the Jordanian government denied that they had ever taken place. In February 1950 rumors that the talks had started again once more led to criticism in the Arab press, and once again Prime Minister Tawfiq Abu al-Huda denied that they were being held. "There is no truth whatsoever," he claimed, "to these rumors. We do intend to discuss changes in the General Armistice Agreement as Article 12 permits. Moreoever, according to the agreement, talks on its amendment are to be held one year after it is signed. If the amendment is agreed on, it will be considered an appendix to the original agreement and it will be valid until a final settlement."[15]

The rumors and al-Tall's accusations were exploited by King 'Abdallah's opponents and some of his supporters as well. Indeed, 'Abdallah's peace efforts met with opposition, or at least reservations, even among his closest advisers. Some of the prominent figures who had reservations—besides Tawfiq Abu al-Huda—were Sa'id al-Mufti and Samir al-Rifa'i, both of whom served as prime minister several times. The Cairo newspaper *al-Zaman* even quoted Sa'id al-Mufti, who was asked to form a new government on April 12, 1950, as saying, "They can cut off my hand but I will not sign a treaty with Israel."[16]

Some of the opposition parties in the West Bank, like al-Ba'th, Al-Qawmiyyun, and al-Tahrir, were extremely hostile to Israel and consequently rejected any attempts at talks or at a political settlement. For al-Qawmiyyun, the publicity about 'Abdallah's negotia-

14. 'Abdallah al-Tall, *Zikhronot 'Abdallah al-Tall* (Tel-Aviv: Ma'arokhot, 1964), p. 314.
15. *HMH* 1 (1950):301.
16. As cited in Ibid., p. 304.

tions with the Israelis served as proof of the Jordanian regime's treason, and they were described as a "scandal".[17]

The pan-Islamic al-Tahrir party, which objected to every attempt by the Jordanian rulers to come to an agreement with Israel, proclaimed that "there is no solution to this problem but the one determined by Islam and laid out by the Qura'n . . . a holy war until Israel no longer exists . . . [this] will save the country which Allah, in blessing it, set aside from the hands of the infidels who will bear the wrath of the master of the world."[18] The party accused King 'Abdallah, Iraqi Prime Minister Nuri al-Sa'id, and Iraqi Crown Prince 'Abd al-Illah of having helped in the establishment of Israel. They were described as traitors worthy of condemnation.

The Jordanian Ba'th expressed a similar view, describing Israel as the fruit of an imperialist plot. "Imperialism," proclaimed al-Ba'th's poster circulated on the anniversary of May 15, "completed the first stage of its plot against the Arab nation when it established the State of Israel and . . . thus brought about barbaric acts and blood-letting and the destruction of the Arab economy."[19] The party argued that even when the Jews and the great powers talk about peace they want it "not because they love peace, but because they need it. . . . Whoever seeks peace from the Arabs must not bring immigrants from all the countries of the world in order to inherit it from the Arabs of Palestine."[20] The rectification of the situation, according to the Ba'th, entailed the destruction of Israel and the restoration of Palestine to the bosom of the Arab world. Any other solution would be considered a failure for the Arab nation.

17. See "al-Sha'b aqwa," poster of July 7, 1958, ISA, File 514–2; G. Broide, "Al-Qawmiyyun al-'arab" [The Arab Nationalists] in "Ha-Miflagot ha-politi-yot ba-Gada ha-Ma'aravit tahat ha-shilton ha-hashemi" [The political parties in the West Bank under the Hashemite regime], ed. Amnon Cohen, mimeo-graphed (Institute of Asian and African Studies, The Hebrew University of Jerusalem, 1972), p. 208.

18. See al-Tahrir's manifesto in R. Simon and A. Landau, "Mifleget ha-shihrur" [The Liberation party], in "Ha-Miflagot ha-politiyot ba-Gada ha-Ma'aravit," p. 616.

19. See ISA, File 681–1; A. Sela, "Mifleget ha-ba'th" [The Ba'th party], in "Ha-Miflagot ha-politiyot ba-Gada ha-Ma'aravit," p. 168.

20. Al-Difa', March 6, 1952.

Not only political groups but also voluntary organizations such as women's organizations and sports clubs in the West Bank supported these attitudes and opinions, demanding that some sort of body be set up to retrieve the "stolen homeland" and rejecting any political settlement with Israel. Thus, for example, the Arab Women's Organization demanded that women be trained so that they could contribute to the national effort for the return of Palestine.[21] One of the sports clubs in Hebron requested that the government help combine military training with its activities in order to prepare the members "to serve the homeland when the time came."[22]

The Palestine Refugees

The attempts by Amman, particularly by King 'Abdallah, to help solve the refugee problem by settling refugees in Jordan and granting them citizenship were strongly opposed by most of the Palestinian leadership in the West Bank and especially by the refugees themselves.

King 'Abdallah was willing to accept the refugees in Jordan partly because he saw in them an economic and political potential that would, as they were gradually absorbed into Jordanian life, contribute to the country's political and economic development. Jordan was even willing to take in refugees who had first gone to other Arab countries. Refugees therefore streamed to Jordan not only from the parts of Palestine ruled by Israel but from the Gaza strip, Egypt, Syria, Lebanon, and Iraq.[23] Rumors about 'Abdallah's attempts to obtain compensation for those who had abandoned property in Israel also encouraged many Palestinian families to emigrate to Jordan.

King 'Abdallah's policy entailed granting the refugees a number of benefits to ease their absorption and to demonstrate the central authorities' willingness to do so. Any refugee could get Jordanian citizenship on request. Refugees were accepted at all levels of public service, some even becoming cabinet members. By fitting the refugee

21. Report dated October 1, 1953, ISA, File 176–8.
22. *Al-Difa'*, June 22, 1953.
23. See Zvi Ne'eman, *Mamlekhet 'Abdullah leahar ha-sipuah* (Jerusalem: Israel Foreign Ministry, 1950), p. 41.

elite into senior public office, 'Abdallah and his followers hoped to strengthen the bonds between the leaders of the populations of both banks.

This policy was opposed by some of the king's ministers as well as by the refugees and the Palestinian opposition leadership. While the former viewed the policy as harmful to Jordan's interests, the Palestinian opponents considered it to be another demonstration of the king's desire to preserve the status quo by weakening, if not erasing completely, the refugees' demand for repatriation.

At that time most of the Jordanian cabinet ministers considered 'Abdallah's "integrationist" policy toward the refugees as liable to cause the kingdom economic and political difficulties. Economically they feared, the policy might be too great a burden on the Jordanian treasury, since the rehabilitation of the refugees required considerable resources. Politically, it was argued that public statements about Jordan's willingness to absorb the refugees might weaken Jordan's bargaining position with Israel, as such declarations were seen to contain a concession to the Jewish state on the refugee problem.[24]

The refugees opposed the Jordanian settlement policy and that of the United Nations Relief and Works Agency (UNRWA) because they saw it as detrimental to their struggle to return to Palestine. "These programs," stated one of the refugee organizations, "have not aimed at fulfilling a pure humanitarian mission but at finally liquidating the Palestine problem by settling the refugees far from their homeland and assimilating them, trying to complete the Jewish imperialist plot and bring the curtain down on the Palestinian tragedy."[25]

When Fawzi al-Mulqi formed his government in May 1953, various refugee groups cabled him their continued opposition to attempts to resettle them inside Jordan. They argued that rehabilitation would take them away from the border areas, thus exposing Jordan to Israeli attack. Anwar al-Khatib, minister of economics and construction in the al-Mulqi government, reacted in this way: "We

24. Ibid., pp. 49–50.
25. See al-Difa', July 20, 1952.

shall do everything [we can] to settle the refugees densely on the West Bank so that they can stand up to the Jewish immigrants now concentrating in new border settlements."[26]

West Bank members of Parliament and other opposition elements also reacted negatively. In a speech at the opening of Parliament on November 1, 1952, Hikmat al-Masri from Nablus, the Palestinian opposition's successful candidate for the speakership, attacked the government's Palestine and refugee policies. "The return of the refugees to their homeland," he argued, "is a sacred duty for all Arabs, especially for the Kingdom of Jordan. . . . The House regrets that this point was not made explicit in the Speech from the Throne. The government must . . . assure them of an honorable life on condition that this does not contradict their natural and legal rights in Palestine and their return to their homeland."[27]

The Jordanian Ba'th party also rejected the refugee rehabilitation programs. It viewed them as part of the plan to clear the way to acceptance of the outcome of the 1948 war, since the maintenance of the refugees' current status, in its opinion, was a thorn in the flesh of Israel, the Arab states, and the great powers because of the threat this situation posed to peace in the Middle East.[28] The Ba'thists thus looked at the refugee problem as part of the overall Palestine problem, the resolution of which depended on the repatriation of the refugees.

The Ba'thists attributed strategic significance to the repatriation of the refugees. It would increase the Arab proportion of the population of Israel, lessen the possibility that Israel could Judaize the country, and prevent Israel from waging war against the Arabs. But the Ba'thists did not merely speak; they also took action to foil the government's plans. They conducted an intensive propaganda campaign in the refugee camps to prevent collaboration

26. *Al-Hayat* (Beirut), June 25, 1953; *HMH* 4 (1953):273.

27. *Filastin,* November 5, 1952.

28. *Filastin,* June 3, 1952. "There are clear signs, though," argues al-Rimawi, "which indicate that as long as the refugee problem continues in its present form, unresolved, it . . . threatens the region, and, as we know, the West is very interested in peace in order to carry out its plans." Ibid.

with UNRWA or with the governmental bodies trying to draw up rehabilitation plans.[29]

The pan-Islamic al-Tahrir, which also opposed the government's rehabilitation program, called on the refugees "to reject every international plan for a solution, even if it is accepted by the U.N. and the Arab states."[30] The party saw as treasonous to the Palestinian cause the United Nations' willingness even to consider a proposal to let the refugees decide whether they wished to return to Palestine or accept compensation in order to settle somewhere else. This was seen as willingness to trade away territory and "turn the problem of liquidating Israel into an economic problem of refugees and compensation."[31] Al-Tahrir argued that repatriation under Jewish rule meant recognition of the Jewish state, and acceptance of compensation indicated willingness to abandon a plot of Muslim land to the infidels. "The question of compensation," it stated, "must be removed from consideration. A homeland is not sold. . . . The acceptance of compensation would be interpreted as conceding our historic rights."[32]

Criticism like this by the Tahrir party, as well as by other political groups, expressed the view, common in the West Bank, that the only solution to the refugee problem was the return to Palestine. The regime in Amman, on the other hand, was inclined to think of resettlement in Jordan and the other Arab states as the solution.

Britain

At least two factors were behind hostility to Britain in the West Bank. One was the policy of the Arab Legion, whose command was British, in border incidents with Israel. The other was the contradiction between Amman's pro-Western stance and the socialist, pan-Arab, or pan-Islamic orientations of the different political parties in the West Bank. The British presence was considered by these parties an obstacle to the realization of their political plans. Consequently, when they criticized the Arab Legion's behavior in the

29. Ibid.
30. From a party statement of February 1, 1960, in Simon and Landau, "Mifleget ha-shihrur," p. 612.
31. Al-Tahrir statement, August 19, 1959; Ibid., p. 611.
32. *Al-Difa'*, December 23, 1951.

1948 war and in the border incidents, they tended to go beyond the specific issue involved and to voice their hostility to the British presence in the kingdom.

The military incidents on the border with Israel during the 1950s and the losses in life and property they caused led the Palestinians to criticize the British command of the Arab Legion, which they thought was restricting the army from going into action against the Israelis. The criticism was heightened by the Legion's strategic military concept, inspired by the British officer corps, according to which the main Jordanian forces were charged with the defense of the East Bank and the inside of the West Bank rather than with the repulsion of Israeli military operations along the border.[33]

The behavior of the Arab Legion and the National Guard in these operations angered the Palestinian opposition. Opposition MPs, especially from the West Bank, demanded that the Legion be given a free hand to react forcefully to Israeli attacks. Qadri Tuqan argued, for example, that "only a daring will and the power of the fist will be able to drive back the frivolous, despicable, and treacherous Jew. As long as the Arabs concede a lot, the Jews will go on running wild."[34] The Ba'thist representative, 'Abdallah Na'was, maintained that "The government must take an unyielding and decisive position to uproot the aggression, which will only be possible with similar reprisals."[35] Opposition circles in the West Bank demanded the removal of the British command from the Arab Legion. They rejected in principle the British-Jordanian defense treaty and other foreign agreements and alliances. Instead, they encouraged military ties with Arab states.[36]

33. For indirect approval of the strategic concept developed by Glubb and of the manner in which the forces were deployed, see John Bagot Glubb, *A Soldier with the Arabs* (London: Hedder and Stoughton, 1957), pp. 314–15.

34. *Filastin,* January 9, 1952.

35. Ibid., January 10, 1952.

36. See, for example, Qadri Tuqan, "Our Only Hope: Renunciation of the Treaty and the Establishment of Arab Unity," *al-Hayat* (Beirut), January 20, 1953. Later, Tuqan would argue that "It must be explained to the Arabs that Jordan will remain a weak link in the Arab world if they do not hasten to strengthen her against treaties, restrictions, and foreign influence." See *Filastin,* October 17, 1953.

In the Ba'thist view, the eradication of British influence from the army was a necessary precondition to weakening British influence in Jordan as a whole and making the Jordanian regime move from a pro-Western to a neutralist orientation. This attitude did not last. Later, in 1956, a pro-Eastern trend emerged strongly in the Ba'th, and it called for cooperation with all Communist states.[37] However, the Ba'th did not explicitly demand that the government give up British financial aid as long as no alternative Arab financing had been found.

Al-Qawmiyyun also rejected the pro-British orientation of Amman. Britain was seen as having conspired in the establishment of Israel. In a statement issued on the anniversary of the adoption of the United Nations partition resolution of November 29, 1947, it accused the British of "a most abominable, criminal act, one of the darkest crimes in human history, a crime of the slaughter of a whole people, a crime the victims of which were a million Arabs expelled from their homes, and seventy million Arabs whose honor was desecrated."[38] Any political and military agreement or alliance between Britain and Jordan was seen by al-Qawmiyyun as perpetuating foreign control and influence by indirect means.

On the same issue, the Jordanian Communist Party considered the British an element that-sowed enmity between Arabs and Jews in Palestine during the Mandate period. The Communists maintained that the British had encouraged the Palestinian Arab leadership to oppose the partition plan in order "to prevent its [Arab Palestine's] independence and . . . an independent state in cooperation with the Jewish people."[39] Britain's efforts to hang on to its political and military influence in the region were, the Communists declared, intended to help create the proper conditions for operations against the Soviet Union. The British were exploiting Israel's aggressive

37. See a report on a Ba'th meeting in Ramallah on September 19, 1956, in which such opinions were voiced; ISA, File 443-3; Sela, "Mifleget ha-ba'th," p. 174.

38. "Al-Sha'b aqwa," December 1957, ISA, File 565-11; Broide, "Al-Qawmiyyun al-'arab," p. 202.

39. See, for example, Communist party poster of June 1952; ISA, File 2872-16; Be'eri, "Megamot seperatistiyot," p. 11.

actions in order to heighten the sense of urgency in forming alliances and military agreements between Britain and the Arab regimes.[40]

It was not only the socialist-oriented political streams that were anti-British; right-wing groups like the Muslim Brotherhood and al-Tahrir also took this position. The Muslim Brotherhood saw foreign—first British and later American—influence in Jordan as a negative factor that retarded the development of the Arab people. The Brotherhood called on the government to dismiss British Colonel John Glubb from his post as commander of the Arab Legion. One day, they argued, the army would have to play its part in the *jihad* against the "infidels"; it was not fitting that an infidel, a British officer, should lead it.[41]

It was not only political considerations that lay behind the Muslim Brotherhood opposition to the British presence; it maintained that this presence also had negative moral effects. The drunkenness and "bad behavior" of the British officers and men serving in Jordan were, it felt, a disgrace. In a notice distributed at a demonstration protesting the dangers the British posed to Muslim morality, the Brotherhood called on the government to purge the Arab Legion of British officers, to close down the dance halls, to forbid the serving of wine on official occasions, and to dismiss the ministers responsible for this policy.[42]

In the opinion of al-Tahrir, which also opposed the British presence, Jordan was more exposed to British influence in domestic and foreign affairs than any other Arab country and followed Britain's orders in everything. Amman's overidentification with British interests even led, the party argued, to a lack of interest on Amman's part in mobilizing for the war against Israel. The party contended that this stance was part and parcel of the regime's

40. On this argument see, for instance, the Communist publication *al-Muqawama al-sha'biyya*, May 1956; Amnon Cohen, "Ha-Miflaga ha-qomunist-it" [The Communist party], in "Ha-Miflagot ha-politiyot ba-Gada ha-Ma'aravit," p. 60.

41. Report dated November 3, 1953, ISA, File 982–16.

42. Poster of August 21, 1957, ISA, File 718–40; R. Simon, "Ha-Ahim ha-muslemim" [The Muslim Brotherhood], in "Ha-Miflagot ha-politiyot ba-Gada ha-Ma'aravit," p. 353.

basic aim of maintaining the separation of the West Bank from the rest of Palestine, so that Amman could keep the West Bank under its own control.[43]

In sum, while opposition groups in the West Bank differed over other issues, they were unanimous in their hostility to Jordan's close ties with Britain. Antagonism to the British presence was shared by the socialist-oriented Ba'thists, by the Communists, and later by al-Qawmiyyun, as well as by the pan-Islamic groupings in the Muslim Brotherhood and al-Tahrir. All of them saw the British presence as the symbol of the Arab world's political, economic, and social inferiority. The British were thus judged, not so much by their deeds as by what they symbolized in the world view of these groups. Yet, despite their expressed attitude, sometimes the opposition groups' actual behavior was much more moderate, partly as a result of the weakness of their bargaining position and their operational capacities vis-à-vis Amman.

Political Organization and Political Representation

Opposition in the West Bank over the issue of political organization stemmed mainly from Amman's desire to shape a policy that would minimize the need for political support from the West Bank. Governmental initiatives like the Emergency Defense Regulations, the Political Parties Law, and the Anti-Communist Law restricted freedom of association and gave the regime broad discretionary powers over political activity and organizations.

The renewal of the defense regulations, which remained in effect after the annexation as a heritage of the British Mandate in Palestine, was scathingly and continuously criticized by the Palestinian opposition in Parliament. Under the regulations, the government had broad authority to restrict the rights of citizens. Political activity could be limited, and any party which, in the conservatives' view, did not serve the "public interest" could be outlawed. The minister of the interior or anyone appointed by him for the purpose had the right to forbid any public assembly if he considered such prohibition vital to the "public interest." The minister was empowered to refuse

43. See R. Simon and A. Landau, "Mifleget ha-shihrur," pp. 589, 591.

to license any publication which, he felt, was detrimental to the
"public interest." These regulations gave the government the authority to arrest or even exile without trial citizens whose activities
were considered by the government to be dangerous to national
security.[44]

The West Bank opposition claimed before the renewal that these
regulations were unconstitutional and raised questions intended
to effect their repeal. In a parliamentary address, the Ba'thist member 'Abdallah al-Rimawi argued that the regulation permitting
the government to exile any citizen without trial was contrary to
the Jordanian Constitution, which states that no citizen may be
deported. He demanded therefore that the regulations be abrogated
and that new ones be adopted that would not restrict citizens'
rights and would be in effect only for the period of an emergency.[45]
Other West Bank representatives showed their dissatisfaction with
the regulations. A memorandum to the prime minister, signed by
fourteen of the twenty West Bank representatives, demanded,
among other things, the release of political prisoners arrested under
the regulations as well as the repatriation of deportees.[46]

The 1954 Political Parties Law and the amended law of 1955 also
reflected the central authorities' wish to influence the nature of
political organization by the opposition on the West Bank. The 1954
law allowed the citizens of Jordan to found political parties as
long as their objectives and regulations were not contrary to the
Constitution. However, the government licensed party activity.
According to the law, the government could dissolve a party if its
views were contrary to the regulations, it presented false details
about its goals, or it was supported by foreign resources. A government decision could be appealed to the High Court of Justice, and
its decision would be final. It also provided that when the law was
promulgated the parties already operating would have to disband
and apply for new licenses.[47]

The 1955 amendments extended the government's power even

44. See *al-Jarida al-Rasmiyya* [The official gazette], August 18, 1954.
45. *Filastin,* December 17, 1952; Sela, "Mifleget ha-ba'th," p. 141.
46. *Al-Hayat* (Beirut), August 2, 1952.
47. *Al-Jarida al-Rasmiyya,* January 17, 1954.

further, permitting it to influence the nature of political organization. Now a government decision to license or refuse to license a political party was final and could not be appealed.[48] Nor, according to the defense ordinance issued by the Ministry of the Interior, did the government have to make public its reasons for granting or refusing licenses or permission to hold political rallies, if it felt that this was not in the public interest.[49] The 1953 Anti-Communist Law imposed additional restrictions on political organization. Any member of a Communist association or any person disseminating propaganda was subject to imprisonment at hard labor. Anyone donating money to a Communist organization or caught selling or distributing literature was liable to from one to three years in prison.[50]

The provisions of the Political Parties Law were used to prevent two parties, the Ba'th and al-Tahrir, from running for Parliament. The Ba'th's application for a license was rejected three times: in February 1952, on the ground that its goals were contrary to the Constitution; in June 1953 and in early 1954, after the passage of the Political Parties Law.[51] Among the reasons the minister of the interior cited for the decision was that the Ba'th founders rejected the existing regime and were a threat to the existence of the state.[52] The Tahrir party presented its request for permission to establish a political party on November 17, 1952. Apparently, there was another request made in January 1953, since the minister of the interior, Sa'id al-Mufti, was studying the party platform at the time. The license was denied, however, on the ground

48. Ibid., April 3, 1955.

49. Al-Difa', August 20, 1955.

50. Al-Jarida al-Rasmiyya, December 16, 1953.

51. On the first request see Filastin, February 11, 1952. The request was presented by 'Abdallah Na'was and Bahjat Abu Gharbiyya, 'Abd al-Rahman Shuqayr, Munif al-Razzaz, Sulayman al-Hadidi, and Farah Ishaq.

On the second request see Ibid., June 24, 1953. On the last one see al-Jihad, March 22, 1954. This time the request was signed by al-Rimawi, Na'was, Abu Gharbiyya, Hamdi 'Abd al-Majid, Husni al-Khuffash, and Farah Ishaq. HMH 3 (1954):207.

52. From a report dated June 28, 1954, ISA, File 413–10; also Sela, "Mifleget ha-ba'th," p. 91.

that the party's principles were incompatible with the Jordanian Constitution.[53]

The government's restrictions on political organizing affected political representation, and this too was a subject of disagreement. Opposition deputies, mainly from the West Bank, consistently and constantly demanded that the government be responsible to Parliament. They also demanded that a vote of no confidence be passed by a simple majority rather than by a special majority of two-thirds. It was not only on the political plane that the representativeness of the system was questioned. There was also criticism from the West Bank of inadequate representation in the administration and the armed services. The feeling of deprivation was made all the more acute by the way the West Bank was discriminated against in the allocation of economic resources for local needs and in the selective recruitment of Palestinians to public service.

In late July 1952, most of the West Bank representatives signed a memorandum accusing the government of favoring East Bankers over West Bankers for military and public office in order to discourage the latter from entering these fields.[54] The Ba'th party, searching for a better balance between the East and West Banks, demanded decentralization of authority among the various government ministries and strengthening of the district offices.[55] It also wanted conscription instituted in order to expand the army. Conscription, however, would have had important ramifications, since it would have made the Palestinization of the army possible for the simple reason that the majority of the population in Jordan after the annexation was Palestinian. Although the demands were rejected, they highlighted the West Bank's dissatisfaction with the limited influence it had on the political decision-making process and its wish to change the situation.

53. The party saw Islam rather than the state as the fundamental principle determining the shape of the political framework. The party also did not recognize the ascriptive principle of inheritance of the throne customary in Jordan, and it called instead for elections to the office of head of state; the principles of the party were considered antagonistic to the Constitution. See *Filastin,* March 10 and 22, 1953; *HMH* 4 (1953):190.

54. *Al-Hayat* (Beirut), August 2, 1952.

55. *Filastin,* October 28, 1952; Sela, "Mifleget ha-ba'th," p. 143.

Freedom of Expression

The restrictions on freedom of expression in the West Bank were evidenced in the closing down of newspapers and the arrest of journalists. On August 1, 1949, for instance, 'Abdallah al-Rimawi and 'Abdallah Na'was, who wrote for the daily newspaper *Filastin,* were arrested for publishing articles critical of the Arab leaders, accusing them of incompetence and intrigues that led to the military defeat of 1948.[56] The severe criticism by West Bank Arabs of the way the Arab Legion's British command conducted the 1948 war and their attacks on the Rhodes agreement led the government to tighten censorship of the press and of the publication of debates in the House of Representatives.

The differences between Prime Minister Tawfiq Abu al-Huda's position and that of the West Bank opposition in late 1952 and early 1953 over the government's foreign and domestic policies led to the closing of West Bank newspapers that supported the opposition. *Filastin,* for instance, was closed down for two days after printing an article insulting to members of the House of Representatives. The Bethlehem monthly *al-Ma'had* was unable to publish for a month because of its criticism of some leaders of Arab states.[57]

These actions received legal authority with the passage of the 1953 Law of Publications by the House of Representatives on September 8, 1953. The law laid down the conditions for publication of a newspaper or journal. The publisher had to have at least a secondary school education; the chief editor had to be at least twenty-three years of age, have an academic education, and could not be a member of the House of Representatives or hold a post in the civil service. A proposed amendment, making five years'

56. *Filastin,* August 8, 1949. The newspaper was closed again for a period of eighteen days in October 1949, because of an article by Kamal Nasir in which he hinted that the telegrams sent to Amman of West Bank support and identification with the Jordanian regime were the result of pressure exerted on the population. See *HMH* 1(1950):149.

57. See *Filastin,* February 4, 1953. On the closure of six newspapers for six months in early 1955, see *Filastin,* February 9, 1955; *HMH* 6 (1955):228.

experience in newspaper editing a possible substitute for higher education, did not pass.[58]

This law was apparently intended to provide a juridical basis for the restrictions on opposition newspapers and journals. The authorities thus hoped to increase their control of opposition representatives like al-Rimawi, Na'was, and Kamal Nasir, who were professional journalists. In fact, in an article printed in *al-Sarih* in September 1953, Na'was attacked the law and referred to it as "one of the plots of reaction." Nor did he spare the members of Parliament who had voted for it. "The Journalist's Association in Jordan," he wrote, "should publish a death notice stating: The Jordanian House of Representatives, most of whose members are ignorant, made so bold as to slaughter the Fourth Estate in the state. . . . this House of Representatives, some of whose members were elected by fraud, bribery, and discrimination, hastened to sentence the freedom of the press to death, to tell the world that the members of the Jordanian House of Representatives are enemies of the free press."[59]

The Law on Sermons and Guidance in Mosques, which made sermons and instruction dependent on written permission from the chief *qadi* (Muslim judge of the religious courts) or his delegate in the districts and subdistricts,[60] also aroused criticism, especially from the Tahrir party and the Muslim Brotherhood, which saw it as a government attempt to tighten control over them. They argued that the law restricted freedom of worship and prevented them from performing religious rites and was therefore contrary to the laws of Islam.[61] The Council of Islamic Law too had reservations about the law and proposed a number of amendments. Apparently

58. *Filastin,* September 9, 1953.

59. *Al-Sarih,* September 12, 1953.

60. Violators of the law were liable to a fine of 10 to 100 dinars and imprisonment for a week to three months. The *qadi* also had the right to revoke the license of a lawbreaker "if it is proved that the public interest requires it." See *al-Jarida al-Rasmiyya,* January 19, 1955.

61. Report dated October 30, 1955, ISA, File 718–40. On arrests among al-Tahrir members for violating the law, see report of February 12, 1955, ISA, File 445–12, and *Filastin,* January 1, 1955.

the reservations of the council, whose tasks included the supervision of preaching and guidance in mosques, stemmed largely from
the fear that its authority would be limited and its position weakened while that of the chief *qadi* would be increased.[62]

Features of the Bargaining Process

The negative attitude of the West Bank Arabs toward Amman on
issues of foreign and domestic policy in the years 1949–54, when
the Palestinians lacked outside support, significantly weakened the
West Bank's bargaining ability for positions of political power and
policymaking. On the other hand, the Palestinians retained a
minimal bargaining power since the possibility of political violence
increased Amman's willingness to cope with the tension through
manipulation rather than by a one-sided, coercive solution. Amman's
policy was based mainly on mechanisms combining elements of
concession, suppression, and compensation.[63] The policy was
possible largely because political awareness and participation in
the West Bank were the preserve of a very narrow social stratum.

The elements of compensation and concession are most clearly
seen in areas of symbolic and expressive significance. Repression
was generally utilized when the regime felt a substantive threat
to its control of the loci of power. By following a policy of concession and compensation, Amman hoped to reach a level of
coexistence with political groups like the National Socialists, the
Muslim Brotherhood, and even, at times, the Ba'thists. Meanwhile,
it tried to suppress extremist groups like the Communists, Hajj
Amin al-Husseini's supporters, and the Tahrir party, which it perceived as threats to its very existence.

The attempt to give the postannexation political system a representative air by instituting elections to the House of Representatives
and assuring the West Bank of equal representation in the Senate as
well as in the House was an instance of the use of compensation.
The appointments policy toward the West Bank was another means
of distributing rewards in order to stave off protest and separatist

62. *Al-Difa'*, January 17, 1955.
63. On the use of similar mechanisms in order to avert a revolution, see
L. Stone, "Theories of Revolution," *World Politics* 28 (1966):107.

orientations. However, the operation of this policy did more than reflect the real power relations between the two banks; it indicated how poor the West Bank's bargaining capabilities were. Amman not only ensured that the West Bank Arabs, despite their majority in the country's population, held no majority in important institutions such as the Senate, the House of Representatives, and the cabinet; it also was very selective in its appointments to politically and militarily powerful posts. Amman tried to select loyal men from families with high social standing and to support the election of cooperative candidates. Many of these candidates came from the Palestinian Nashashibi family, one of the leading families in the Palestinian community during the Mandate, and from its adherents, who had cooperated with King 'Abdallah and helped mobilize support for annexation among the Palestinian Arabs.

The Nashashibi faction figured prominently in appointments to the Senate in the first years after annexation. Of the eight West Bank Arabs appointed to the Senate after annexation five were Nashashibi supporters: Raghib al-Nashashibi; Sulayman Tuqan, who served as mayor of Nablus; Sulayman Taji al-Faruqi, originally from Ramleh; Farid Arshayyid, a notable from Jenin; and Hussein Khawajah, from Lydda. Other members of the first Senate were Sheikh Muhammad 'Ali al-Ja'bari, mayor of Hebron, and Wadi' Da'mas, Christian mayor of Beit Jalla, who had worked for the annexation of the West Bank. The only person not a member of the Nashashibi group was 'Abd al-Latif Salah from Lydda who became an open opponent of the Husseini family (the Nashashibi's rivals) after annexation.[64]

'Abd al-Latif Salah's case demonstrated King 'Abdallah's tendency to use the appointment policy to placate or co-opt his rivals from time to time. Another such case was that of Khlusi Khayri, who was a member of the opposition Ba'th until 1952 when he joined the government as minister of economics and development in six of the next ten cabinets. Anwar Nusayba, from Jerusalem, a member of the Husseini camp and a former secretary of the all-Palestine

---

64. *HMH* 1 (1950):302; Clinton Bailey, "The Participation of the Palestinians in the Politics of Jordan" (Ph.D. diss., Columbia University, 1966), p. 102.

government in Gaza, was given a place in the new administration. So too was Hussein Fakhri al-Khalidi, who had formerly been a sharp critic of 'Abdallah's Palestine policy.[65] Nevertheless, most of the appointees came from Palestinian families considered long-time supporters of the regime. The fifteen cabinets that served from April 24, 1950, until October 29, 1956, all included Palestinian men, many of whom had close ties with the Nashashibi camp and were members of families of high standing in the West Bank.[66]

In the Jordanian cabinet, West Bankers held most of the economic portfolios—rehabilitation, construction, economy, and trade—almost continuously. The clearly economic nature of these portfolios and their dependence on the court's decisions in key economic issues, however, generally made it possible to neutralize their political potential and prevent their being turned into loci of political power independent of the court. Sometimes in order to still complaints that they were not party to important decisions, West Bank Arabs were compensated by being given the foreign and defense portfolios as well. However important these ministries may have been, they did not constitute the real loci of power in Jordan.

The appointment of Palestinians to Jordanian military service was even more selective. Since the Arab Legion was a volunteer army, the central authorities could control the selection of recruits as they saw fit; volunteers could easily be accepted or rejected. Selection was guided by the principle that a hard core of elite regiments composed of Bedouin troops loyal to Amman had to be maintained.[67] Thus, despite the appointment and recruitment of Palestinians to the Arab Legion after annexation, the basic policy of the Jordanian army command did not change and ensured the Bedouin character of infantry regiments and motorized units. Indeed, from 1953 to 1956 seven of the Legion's eighteen regiments were overwhelmingly composed of Bedouin. Most of the recruits

65. Ibid., p. 98.
66. Ibid.
67. P. J. Vatikiotis, *Politics and the Military in Jordan* (London: Frank Case, 1967), pp. 17, 26–29.

from the West Bank served as technicians, and those who served with the infantry regiments were not generally combat soldiers.[68] So while trying to appease the opposition by recruiting Palestinians to the army, the central authorities encouraged the concentration of loyal elements in key positions and in elite combat units. This helped Amman preserve its control of the army despite the annexation.

In the realm of foreign policy, Amman tried to appease the opposition elements with statements couched in political symbols and values acceptable to them. In late 1949, for instance, 'Abdallah attacked the partition of Palestine. In visits to both banks between October 15 and 18, he firmly declared that as long as he lived he would do everything in his power to prevent partition.[69] Behind the scenes, however, he was negotiating a political settlement with Israel. The Annexation Act also stressed the regime's commitment to work for the restoration of Palestine to the Arabs, although this was not backed by actual government policy.

Tawfiq Abu al-Huda, who served as prime minister several times during the 1950s and represented the conservative faction among the regime's supporters, was diligent in making political declarations almost identical with those current in West Bank political circles. In a speech delivered on June 8, 1954, in which he presented the government's program, he proclaimed: "The government stresses that there is no peace and that there are no negotiations with the Jews and that any attempt to change this policy will have no impact. . . . The refugees are owners and allies of the land. The government will work to assure them of an honorable life and to preserve their rights in international organizations, until they regain their rights in full."[70] This speech however was more an act of symbolic compensation by the government aimed at its West Bank opponents, who opposed Tawfiq Abu al-Huda's appointment as prime minister, than a guideline for policy.

It was in legislation that the regime made its most striking conces-

68. Ibid., pp. 82–93.
69. *HMH* 1 (1950):148.
70. *HMH* 5 (1954):294.

sions. Opposition members of the House of Representatives, most of whom were from the West Bank, were able to propose amendments to the Constitution and even pass new laws limiting the government's broad authority. In fact, the 1952 Constitution emphasized the government's responsibility to the legislature and limited its freedom in matters of finance and foreign policy; treaties or contracts involving a territorial change or a financial commitment had to be ratified by the House of Representatives. The Constitution also limited the king's right to veto decisions of the House.

From May 1953 to May 1954, during the term of the liberal Fawzi al-Mulqi as prime minister, there were further constitutional amendments proposed emphasizing the subordination of the executive to the legislature. The most important amendment would have forced the resignation of a government after a vote of no confidence passed by a simple majority of members instead of by the two-thirds majority specified in the Constitution.[71] Articles were added to the Constitution, even over cabinet objections, concerning the length of time a government could stay in office after losing a no confidence motion and forbidding members of a caretaker government from running in the elections. Proposed alliances and treaties would have to be ratified by both houses of Parliament.[72] On January 30, 1954, the Senate passed the proposed amendments, and the government decided not to bring the matter before the Special Council for clarification of the law, although it considered that Parliament's action was *ultra vires,* since the Constitution specified that no articles could be added to it.[73]

However, legislative concessions by the government were mainly of symbolic value and intended only as palliatives to the Palestinian opposition. The 1955 amended Political Parties Law, for instance,

71. Ibid., p. 206.

72. Other demands included: legislation about trade unions and political parties, the separation of the military and the police, and the transfer of authority over the latter to the Ministry of the Interior. See *Filastin,* May 25, 1953.

73. On the government decision see Ibid., February 6, 1954; *HMH* 5 (1954): 206.

stressed the government's broad authority and its superiority to Parliament despite any constitutional limitations imposed on it. These symbolic concessions, however, helped Amman to live with the conflict rather than try to confront the opposition, which would then have sought an unequivocal decision. On the other side, the opposition could point to its symbolic deeds as evidence of its role in redefining the interests of the Jordanian regime.[74]

One can argue that the variety of patterns of manipulation and the persistence of the struggle between the different political groups in the West Bank allowed Amman to differentiate among the opposition parties and increase the possibilities of internal conflicts among them. The ability to manipulate and redefine ambiguous symbols thus enabled the regime to reduce the conflict between the two banks without giving up important positions.

The inability of the Palestinians to bargain effectively with Amman in the years 1948–54 derived also from their constant indecision between one aim and its diametric opposite. Their will to ensure their physical survival by cooperating to some extent politically and economically with Amman helped the tendency toward indecisiveness to grow. Many of the Palestinians in the West Bank preferred not to play up the protracted struggle with the regime but rather to take the path of personal mobility in preference to the promotion of collective goals. They were willing to accept partial accomplishments rather than try to attain radical change through constant struggle.

The fact that the tension between Amman and the Palestinian opposition groups did not lead to extremist action at this time (1949–54) indicates that, rather than wishing to set up a new regime, the Palestinians were interested in articulating their objections to the existing one and bringing about a political revision within it. One might recall 'Abdallah Na'was's distinction that the Ba'th supported a reformist rather than a revolutionary approach to social and political problems.[75] Thus, notwithstanding its dissatis-

74. On the use of symbolization to moderate conflict, see Lewis Coser, *Continuities in the Study of Social Conflict* (New York: Free Press, 1967), pp. 37–51.
75. See *al-Ba'th,* February 21, 1950.

faction with the regime and its desire to establish a democratic, socialist republic in time, the Ba'th was willing to cooperate with Amman, at least on an ad hoc basis. The Ba'thists also argued that a party's strength is determined not only by its ability to attain its goals while participating in government, but also by its skill in criticizing and overseeing the government's activities as an opposition party.[76]

Da'ud Hamdan, one of the Tahrir party's top leaders, expressed a similar thought: "We shall not make propaganda for the use of force in order to establish an Islamic state. But we shall see to it that Muslims understand Islam, until the Islamic faith grows among them."[77] Even the Communists—as Amnon Cohen argues—did not take action to destroy the regime in Jordan. Moreover, from the beginning of the 1950s, they moved away from separatism and tended more and more to recognize the existence of both banks within a single political framework.[78]

The West Bank may have been weak in bargaining with Amman between 1949 and 1954, but it was not entirely powerless. Amman's desire to legitimate its rule in the West Bank, combined with the view held by some of the West Bank political parties that the political solution was only temporary, encouraged the latter to use conditional legitimacy as a political resource. Whether they granted or denied legitimacy to Amman depended partly on the extent to which they were allowed to participate in the political process and to influence it. Given the fact that Amman's desire was not only to succeed in keeping the Palestinians away from positions of political decision-making but also to establish a political system permitting long-term coexistence with them, its willingness to accept cooperative relations between the banks in the form of conditional legitimacy becomes understandable.

76. See Bahjat Abu Gharbiyya in *Filastin,* January 23, 1952.

77. Statement on May 2, 1954, ISA, File 2705–4; Simon and Landau, "Mifleget ha-shihrur," p. 488.

78. See Cohen, "Political Parties in the West Bank under the Hashemite Regime," in *Palestinian Arab Politics,* ed. Moshe Ma'oz (Jerusalem: Jerusalem Academic Press, 1975), p. 31.

CRISIS IN CONDITIONAL LEGITIMACY

The pattern of conditional legitimacy was severely undermined in 1957. Fearing the growing intervention of Syria and Egypt and their massive influence on the Palestinian opposition, the Jordanian court decided to maintain its control by taking a hard line against the opposition. The dismissal in April 1957 of the Sulayman al-Nabulsi cabinet, which was composed of opposition parties, and the king's refusal to yield to the pressure exerted on him by the supporters of these parties marked the beginning of a legitimacy crisis in Amman-West Bank relations.[79] After the cabinet was dismissed, the Ba'thists, National Socialists, and Communists, including independent members of Parliament, organized themselves into "national committees" in various West Bank cities. These were to spearhead operations aimed at forcing the Nabulsi government's return to power. The committees drew up petitions and organized demonstrations against the court.[80] More than that, high-ranking army supporters of the opposition parties resorted to illegal activities like the attempted coup at Zarqa on April 13.[81]

However, the king showed no willingness to compromise with, let alone yield to, the opposition. On April 25 martial law was proclaimed throughout the land. Emergency regulations were implemented, political parties disbanded, and many of the activists

79. On the decision of the king to dismiss the Nabulsi government, which was accused of being under Communist influence, see King Hussein, *Uneasy Lies the Head* (London: Heinemann, 1962), p. 133.

80. On April 22, 1957, demonstrators in Nablus, Ramallah, and Jerusalem called on the authorities to reinstate the Nabulsi government and to cease the interrogations of and to release the army officers suspected of anti-regime activity. See the report dated June 25, 1957, ISA, File 457-9. See also the "National Committees" poster published on April 11, 1957, calling on the king to continue their liberal domestic policy, to strengthen ties with Egypt and Syria, and to support the policy of positive neutrality. *Filastin,* April 12, 1957.

81. For details on the first attempt to overthrow the monarchy that occurred at Zarqa on April 13, 1957, see Hussein, *Uneasy Lies the Head,* pp. 140–46; *al-Hayat* (Beirut), April 16, 1957. Among those who took part in the plot and found refuge in Syria were the chief of staff, 'Ali Abu Nuwar, and the chief of military intelligence, Mahmud Musa.

arrested. Under the emergency regulations, the defense minister was given the status of military governor-general and authorized to suppress any activity liable to endanger public security and to appoint military governors in all parts of the country. The government also used its authority to dismiss municipal councillors and appoint replacements. The city councils of Nablus, Tulkarm, Bethlehem, Zarqa, Amman, and Madaba were removed and special committees were appointed to run the affairs of the communities.[82]

The disbanding of the parties; the purge of the parliamentary opposition; and the flight of some of the leadership to Syria marked the start of a period, which was to last until 1961, when the opposition was suppressed to such an extent that it was quite ready to resort to violence. This readiness was reinforced by the new pan-Arabism in Cairo and Damascus which served as a source of ideological inspiration as well as material support for the Palestinian opposition. This encouraged the Palestinians to try to fulfill their goals through the pan-Arab option despite the risk of confrontation with Amman. The delicate balance of conditional legitimacy was upset.

Pan-Arabism up to then had been conceived of as a relationship based on mutual recognition of each Arab state's right to sovereignty. The Nasirist regime introduced a new approach that stressed political unity. It was an attempt to radicalize pan-Arabism by liquidating the separate political states and concentrating the instrumental and ideological bonds of the Arab populations in a single political unit. Jordan, in contrast, tended toward a confederal conception of unity with strict respect for the sovereignty of each state.[83] The Syrian-Egyptian union of February 1, 1958, and the Arab Federation of Jordan and Iraq, proclaimed on February 14, 1958, reflected these two differing concepts.

The Nasirist regime was aggressive in its efforts to implement as well as to justify its approach, even if it meant bypassing the Arab

82. See *al-Difa'*, May 23 and 30, 1957; *HMH* 8 (1957):309. For the decree disbanding the parties see *al-Jarida al-Rasmiyya,* May 16, 1957.

83. On the difference between the Egyptian and the Jordanian concepts of Arab unity see, for instance, the correspondence between President Nasir and King Hussein in *Middle Eastern Affairs* 12 (1961):142–48.

governments and intervening in their domestic affairs. "Three years ago, when we began to instruct our military attachés in the Arab capitals to increase activity which is not strictly diplomatic," President Nasir declared, according to a Jordanian source, "one of the Egyptian ambassadors came to me and said: 'I have heard about the military instructions you have given the military attachés. If it is true, I am afraid we shall find ourselves in conflict with all the Arab states.' I answered him: 'My dear friend, it is not shameful or beneath one's dignity to work for Egypt. If the operations of our attachés are discovered, the world will say that Egypt is doing her duty and she is free to choose the means she thinks are suitable. . . .' We can only say that we have accomplished our mission when the last vestiges of imperialism are wiped out and we ensure that the institutions of government are in Arab hands, friendly to Egypt, and that they operate in accord with our interests and are willing to do as we ask."[84]

Nasir therefore tried to increase his influence among the opposition groups in the West Bank in order to gain their cooperation even if this meant violence against the Jordanian regime. Connections between Cairo and Damascus and the opposition parties in the West Bank were strengthened by visits of Syrian delegations, composed mainly of Ba'thists, to the West Bank, usually Nablus and Tulkarm. In March 1956, for instance, six delegations with a total of 500 members visited Nablus and met with members of the Ba'th, the National Socialist party, and al-Qawmiyyun. Some of the visitors even participated in demonstrations taking place in West Bank cities, such as one in Nablus on May 15, 1956, the Israeli Independence Day.[85]

The opposition elements on both banks stepped up their cooperation with Cairo and Damascus after the attempted coup in Zarqa. The flight abroad of Palestinian opposition leaders like 'Abdallah al-Rimawi, Ya'qub Zia al-Din, 'Abdallah Na'was, Bahjat Abu Gharbiyya, Kamal Nasir, and 'Abd al-Muhsin Abu Mezhar, as well as of senior officers like 'Ali Abu Nuwar and 'Ali al-Hiyari, led to the

84. See *al-Difa'*, July 3, 1957.
85. See report dated May 16, 1956, ISA, File 653–10; Sela, "Mifleget ha-ba'th," p. 104.

formation of a Jordanian Revolutionary Council in Damascus, with the assistance of the head of Syrian military intelligence, 'Abd al-Hamid al-Sarraj.[86] The council operated in coordination with Egypt and Syria to overthrow the Jordanian monarchy. It began gathering military and political information about Jordan and recruiting and training local people in preparation for the anticipated coup.[87] Meanwhile plans were made for terrorist attacks to be carried out throughout the kingdom.[88] Arms smuggled from Syria were discovered in Nablus and Tubas and in a refugee camp near Amman. Those who were arrested because of such activity received financial aid from the council. The exiled leadership and military officers thus acted as a link between Syria and Egypt and their Jordanian, mainly West Bank, supporters.

Attempts were also made to establish a revolutionary vanguard among Jordanians studying at Syrian and Egyptian universities. More fertile soil was found among Jordanian teachers who had studied at the Damascus and Beirut universities as external students and went there for their examinations during the summer. They too were subjected to propaganda, and attempts were made to recruit them. In 1959, the Ba'th and al-Qawmiyyun founded the National Students Organization, which was to be their front organization. But cooperation between the Ba'th and al-Qawmiyyun was not restricted to winning hearts and minds. Together they planned the assassination of major political figures such as Samir al-Rifa'i, Hazza' al-Majali, Bahjat al-Talhuni, and Sherif Nasir bin Shakir in prepara-

---

86. On the cooperation between the Jordanian exiles and Syrian intelligence, see reports dated May 15, 1958, and August 25, 1958, ISA, File 425–7.

87. On the uncovering of the intelligence network made up mostly of Ba'thists, see report dated December 16, 1958, ISA, File 775–8. On recruitment attempts, see testimony of a Bethlehem teacher according to a report dated August 26, 1958, ISA, File 425–7; and Sela, "Mifleget ha-ba'th," pp. 106–07.

88. Indeed the number of attacks increased in 1957; there were attacks on the United States Information Agency Office in Amman, on the Turkish embassy, and on the Amman electricity plant. There were also attempts to destroy bridges and telephone lines. Bombs were laid at ministers' houses and assassination attempts were made against the king. *HMH* 9 (1958):85.

tion for the coup that would bring Jordan into the United Arab Republic (UAR).[89]

Apparently there were three attempts made to overthrow the regime between 1958 and 1960. The first, headed by Colonel Mahmud al-Rusan, was supposed to take place in the summer of 1958. The Jordanian authorities uncovered the plot and arrested him and most of the agents who had infiltrated from Syria. The second attempt was headed by the Deputy Chief of Staff Sadiq al-Shara' and Brigadier Adib Qasim and was scheduled to take place in July 1959. A great deal of time was spent on the preparatory work, and the opposition leaders inside Jordan were informed of the plan. Again, the security forces managed to learn of the plot, and most of the conspirators were arrested. The third attempt was made in mid-1960. The plotters were led by the former head of the Arab Legion intelligence services, Colonel Qasim Muhammad al-Nasir. Bahjat Abu Gharbiyya of the Ba'th party was sent from Damascus to Jordan to organize his party for its role in the coup. This attempt too was nipped in the bud, and the conspirators were arrested.[90]

Meanwhile, Syrian and Egyptian radio conducted an intensive propaganda campaign against the Jordanian regime with the aim of inciting the Palestinians in Jordan against it. The king was accused of contacts with Israel, of secret meetings on the border with Israeli Prime Minister David Ben-Gurion, and of conducting a policy inimical to Arab interests. A lot of air time was also devoted to reports of terrorist action in Jordan—the blowing up of ministers' houses and attacks on public places.[91]

Thus, unlike the years 1949–54, when Amman–West Bank relations were characterized by conditional legitimacy, 1957 to 1961

89. For details on weapon training for student members, see report dated February 4, 1959, ISA, File 424–1; Sela, "Mifleget ha-ba'th," p. 98. On their assassination plan, see report dated November 13, 1958, ISA, File 1021–4.

90. On the first attempt see *Middle East Record* 1 (1960):327. Hereafter cited as *MER*. On the second and third attempts see *al-Jihad*, May 22 and 25, 1959.

91. *MER* 1 (1960):148–50.

can be considered a period of legitimacy crisis. In both periods the gulf between the political goals of the two parties was deep and the bargaining as well as the exchange process between them tended to be weak. However, in the earlier period the confederal perception of inter-Arab relations made it easier for Amman to adopt a policy intended to reduce conflict in order to preserve the pattern of conditional legitimacy. But in the latter period, when intervention by Cairo and Damascus in West Bank politics increased, Jordan considered its attempts to compensate the opposition groups dangerous enough to threaten its very existence. It thus had fewer qualms about a confrontation with the West Bank despite the assistance the latter received from outside.

3

Legitimacy and Concession
(1955–1957 and 1961–1967)

THE GROWTH OF CONDITIONAL LEGITIMACY

A more integrative concept of Arab unity emerged during the years 1955 to 1957 and 1961 to 1967 which allowed radical Arab regimes to intervene in Jordanian domestic politics. Confidence rose among the Palestinians in their ability to influence Amman and affect decision-making.

These same new circumstances made it difficult for Amman to continue a policy of unilateral control over the West Bank without risking critical confrontation both with its political opposition and with the radical Arab regimes. A policy of limited concessions became necessary in order to maintain coexistence with the Palestinians. This was the main issue of Amman's politics after the mid-1950s. The search for a balance among conflicting pressures and cooperative interests reflected the choice between two alternatives: resorting to force and responding positively to the opposition's demands. This dilemma confronted Amman in connection with the Baghdad Pact, the firing of British General John Bagot Glubb, the appointment of the Nabulsi government, and the issue of the "Palestinian entity."

The Baghdad Pact

The Baghdad Pact, one of the first manifestations of an integrative concept of Arab unity, came into being in late February 1955, when

Iraq signed a military agreement with Turkey and Pakistan.[1] This
was in line with a British policy to protect its political interests in
the Middle East by promoting military alliances with and among
some of the countries there. Other Arab states were invited to join.
Saudi Arabia, Yemen, and Egypt opposed the pact; Lebanon took
a neutral position; and Syria and Jordan, vacillating and hesitating
over what course to choose, were exposed to pressures from both
sides. Egypt and Iraq then became major rivals.

Nadav Safran argues that the Egyptian-Iraqi conflict over the
Baghdad Pact was not the result of ideological differences regarding
the correct political orientation for the Arab world, since both
were pro-Western. Rather, the conflict reflected their struggle for
leadership of the Arab states. In the course of time, however, they
concealed their power struggle behind an ideological cover. President
Nasir opposed the pact not so much to protect Egyptian interests
as to promote pan-Arab ones. "It was natural for Nasser," writes
Safran, "to attack his opponents for breaking up Arab solidarity,
as envisaged in the Arab League Pact, for exaggerating the Soviet
and communist danger in order to justify his misdeed, for pretending
falsely that his move would help the Palestinian cause, and for
arguing against the true wishes and interests of his own people and
the Arabs generally. All these themes were logical weapons for Nasser to employ in fighting for *Egypt's* interest; but they all happened
also to be themes that appealed greatly to the Arabs."[2]

By putting the issue in this light, Nasir justified Egypt's mobilization of Arab public opinion and the behavior of political groups
which opposed the pact in order to take action against their own
governments. This opposing pressure succeeded relatively easily in
Syria, where Faris al-Khuri's government gave way to a government
of leftists, neutralists, and pan-Arabists who sided with Egypt. The
struggle in Jordan was tougher.

Jordan's initial desire to join the pact was accelerated by promises,
mainly of military aid, given to King Hussein by Britain. In early

1. See "Pact (Baghdad) of Mutual Cooperation: Turkey and Iraq," in
Diplomacy in the Near and Middle East: A Documentary Record, ed. J. C.
Hurewitz, 2 vols. (Princeton: D. Van Nostrand, 1956), 2:390–91.

2. See Nadav Safran, *From War to War* (New York: Pegasus, 1969), p. 80.

December 1955, General Sir Gerald Templer, chief of the Imperial General Staff, arrived in Amman to try to persuade the government to accede to the pact. He promised that the British subsidy to the Arab Legion would be increased from £10 million in 1955 to £16.5 million the first year after Jordan joined and to £12.5 million every year thereafter. He also promised aid to expand the infantry by 25 percent and the Jordanian Air Force "as fast as pilots could be trained."[3]

The opposition parties tried to thwart the government's plans by actively supporting the policy of Egypt, Syria, and Saudi Arabia. President Nasir found supporters in the National Socialist party, the National Front (Communists), the Ba'th, al-Qawmiyyun, and even the Muslim Brotherhood, all of which had at first operated mainly in the West Bank. Their activity chiefly consisted of distributing propaganda favoring resistance to any attempt by Jordan to accede to the pact.[4] Some of the opposition deputies, such as Hikmat al-Masri, Ahmad al-Da'ur, and 'Abd al-Qadir Salih, demanded political union with Egypt. Egypt and Saudi Arabia provided financial aid to the antipact struggle in Jordan. Part of the money was spent bribing influential people to support the opposition. Some was given to Jordanian daily newspapers, "members of Parliament, agitators, or anyone else from whom they needed help."[5] The Syrian Ba'th party also helped finance its Jordanian sister party, while the Communist party and the National Front were aided by money from the Soviet embassy in Damascus.[6]

Not only opposition groups but also Palestinians who had been considered pro-Jordanian were influenced by Egypt on this issue. For example, 'Azmi al-Nashashibi, Na'im 'Abd al-Hadi, 'Ali Husna, and Sam'an Da'ud, all Palestinians who were appointed to Sa'id

3. John Bagot Glubb, *A Soldier with the Arabs* (London: Hedder and Stoughton, 1957), p. 393.

4. See, for instance, the publication entitled, "Al-Ittifaq al-Turqi al-Iraqi" [The Turkish-Iraqi agreement] of February 1955, where the pact's supporters had been called "agents of Imperialism and enemies of the national struggle for the liberation of Palestine." ISA, File 493–10.

5. See Glubb, *A Soldier,* p.294.

6. Clinton Bailey, "The Participation of the Palestinians in the Politics of Jordan" (Ph.D. diss., Columbia University, 1966), p. 176.

al-Mufti's cabinet in May 1955, agreed to Jordan's accession to the pact contingent on Egypt's approval of a counterproposal formulated by the Jordanian government for the negotiations with Iraq and Britain.[7] When the Palestinian ministers' request was rejected by the cabinet, they resigned and were followed by the entire cabinet.

Efforts by the new Jordanian government formed by Hazza' al-Majali in December to bring Jordan into the alliance also failed. His proposal that negotiations with Britain about the pact be resumed in due time led to five days of stormy demonstrations in Amman and in West Bank cities. The demonstrators threatened that the West Bank would secede from the kingdom if the government decided to sign the pact. Consulates of states supporting the pact were attacked, UNRWA offices in Jerusalem were razed, and Musa al-'Alami's farm near Jericho was damaged by refugees from nearby camps. Six of al-Majali's ministers resigned, and on December 20 he followed them.[8]

The Jordanian government's policy toward the Baghdad Pact, which moved from intensive attempts to join it to the decision not to do so, reflected the increased ability of the opposition parties to bargain with and to gain concessions from Amman. Amman's capability to get Jordan into the pact was affected not only by the strengthening of the Palestinian political parties on the West Bank but also by the increased political involvement of broader sectors of the West Bank population. Appealing to the West Bank public over the head of the government, the Syrian and Egyptian regimes helped to distribute political power among the Palestinian masses. Consequently, Amman found it difficult to continue to handle the conflict with the West Bank solely through contact with West Bank political leaders. The regime now had to look for a new common denominator, one that would satisfy the newly active groups and individuals in the West Bank.

The greater the degree of public participation by the Palestinian population, the more restricted the maneuverability of the West

7. See *al-Hayat* (Beirut), January 14, 1956.

8. For more details see *al-Jihad* and *al-Difa'*, December 12–22, 1955; *HMH* 7 (1956):130.

Bank political leadership, which now had to demonstrate more accomplishments to a wider audience than it had had to deal with in the past. The political events surrounding the Baghdad Pact not only deeply affected Palestinian behavior in the West Bank but also contributed to Amman's decision to maintain coexistence between the two banks through concessions rather than through oppression.

Glubb's Dismissal

The dismissal of General John Bagot Glubb and thirty-six senior British officers from the Arab Legion on March 1, 1956, is another example of how the regime made concessions to the opposition parties and strengthened the pattern of coexistence. King Hussein explained the dismissal quite simply. He wanted to give the command to Jordanian officers with modern military training. "I was determined," stated the king, "to build up strong, well-balanced armed forces. . . . Our self-respect demanded that we fight our battles alone."[9] He also opposed Glubb's strategic plan, should war break out with Israel, to withdraw the army beyond the Jordan River and thus abandon the West Bank.

Actually the dismissal was more complicated. The king did not deny that the pressure of domestic public opinion and Arab opinion outside Jordan was also a factor.[10] Glubb's dismissal was regarded popularly as a symbol of Jordan's release from its close bond with Britain. The dismissal enhanced the king's public image and reinforced his standing in the Jordanian officer corps, which had been demanding more responsibility and key positions.

The move was welcomed by both the king's supporters and his opponents. The Ba'th party, for instance, organized an enthusiastic demonstration in Nablus in support of the action. Public associations such as the National Union of Jordanian Women voiced their sup-

9. King Hussein, *Uneasy Lies the Head* (London: Heinemann, 1962), p. 113.

10. Ibid., p. 118. Glubb himself says that the demands for his dismissal, especially from the Ba'th party, became stronger after 1954 against the backdrop of the Israeli military activity along the border with Jordan. See Glubb, *A Soldier*, p. 431.

port. The dismissal was not perceived as of narrow significance, involving only changes in military staff. It was regarded by the opposition as an action against politically and economically influential foreign powers and a necessary step toward closer Jordanian association with radical Arab regimes.[11] Amman's success in using the dismissal to gain the support of opposing political factions compensated for its failure to prevent the victory of its opponents in the Baghdad Pact case. Both the pact and the dismissal show how easy it was to mobilize a broad Arab public consensus over an issue of foreign policy, particularly one involving an element as unpopular as Britain.

The decision to fire Glubb, like Amman's decision not to join the Baghdad Pact, can be seen as a concession to the repeated demands by the opposition for a change in Jordan's pro-Western stance. These demands grew stronger and more insistent after the mid-1950s as the opposition strengthened its links to radical Arab regimes.

The Nabulsi Government

The decision of the royal court not to interfere in the election of 1956, which brought the opposition parties to power, and the appointment of Sulayman al-Nabulsi, the leader of the National Socialists, as prime minister provides another illustration of the attempt of the regime to deal with the opposition's demands through concession. This case, however, differed fundamentally from preceding ones in critical respects. Previously the regime had given largely symbolic concessions to the opposition parties while maintaining power. This time Amman had to yield real power.

The court's concessions in the Baghdad Pact affair and in the Glubb case had a cumulative impact on the political behavior of the opposition. Politically, the opposition leaders learned that, with the support of radical Arab regimes, they could press Amman to reconsider and reorder its political priorities. Glubb's dismissal also exposed the Jordanian army to more radical Arab influence and therefore permitted it to become increasingly politicized. The

11. For a Ba'thist poster expressing this mood, see report dated March 14, 1956, ISA, File 681–9.

Legion was placed under the Egyptian-controlled Arab Joint Command in October 1956, enabling political groups to proselytize among the officers on behalf of ideas that were often contrary to those of the regime.[12]

Against this background, the opposition agitated for more extensive changes in Jordan's relations with the Arab countries, the Communist countries, and the Western world. Changes were implemented by the pro-Egyptian Nabulsi cabinet, which was made up of National Socialists, the Ba'th, the National Front, and three independents.[13] The six National Socialist ministers held the key portfolios, including the offices of prime minister, foreign minister, and ministers of defense and interior. A Ba'thist served as minister of state for foreign affairs and a National Front member as minister of agriculture. The development, transport, and finance portfolios went to independents.[14]

The platform presented by the new government pointed to the expected changes in foreign as well as in domestic policy. In domestic policy, the government promised to repeal the laws restricting the freedom of the individual and to introduce conscription.[15] In foreign policy, the government declared its adherence to economic and military agreements with the Arab countries and its desire for federal union as the basis for a comprehensive Arab unity. It took the position that Jordan could not survive indefinitely as a separate political entity but must be bound militarily, economically, and politically to other Arab states. "My government"— proclaimed al-Nabulsi—"intends to work for federal union with the free Arab states because without such a union . . . we will not be

12. On the establishment of the Joint Arab Command by Egypt, Syria, and Jordan on October 24, 1956, and the appointment of Marshall 'Abd al-Hakim 'Amir as commander, see *al-Ahram* (Cairo), October 26, 1956.

13. There were 144 candidates running for office in this election. The National Socialists won 12 seats in the House of Representatives; the Ba'th won 2; the National Front, 3; the Muslim Brotherhood, 4; and the Tahrir party, 1. There were 8 members from the Arab Constitutional party and 10 independents. See *al-Difa'*, October 22, 1956; *HMH* 8 (1957):145.

14. The ministers of labor, economics, agriculture, and development and the minister of state for foreign affairs were West Bank residents. Ibid.

15. See *al-Difa'*, October 28, 1956.

able to carry out our desires."[16] At the same time, it abrogated the military treaty with Britain and considered the House of Representatives' recommendation for establishment of diplomatic relations with the USSR.

Britain was not the only victim of the anti-Western policy of the new government. A National Socialist party meeting in Nablus on October 24, 1956, called on the government to break off economic, cultural, and political relations with France because of its policy in Algeria. Members of other parties joined the cry and even called for a general strike on October 28.[17] Parliament ratified the government's decision on November 1, 1956, to break off relations with France.

Reservations about the United States were apparent in the Nabulsi government's demand that supervision of American economic projects in Jordan be made its responsibility.[18] Anti-Americanism was reflected in the government's rejection of the Eisenhower Doctrine of January 1957, which aimed to forestall Communist intervention in Middle East countries. The minister of state for foreign affairs, 'Abdallah al-Rimawi, argued that the doctrine was intended to strengthen Israel by maintaining the political status quo and by getting the Arabs to recognize the Jewish state.[19]

The Nabulsi government's closer relations with Egypt and its support of Nasir's policy of positive neutralism made rapprochement with the Communist countries easier. The Jordanian press began to make plain its sympathy for the USSR, particularly after the Suez War between Israel and Egypt in 1956. "We regard the Russian warnings to the three attacking states [Britain, France, and Israel]," argued the editor of *Filastin*, "as the help of a friend

16. On this argument see Sylayman al-Nabulsi's interview in *Filastin*, March 26, 1957.

17. See *Filastin*, October 27, 1956.

18. *Filastin*, January 17, 1957; *HMH* 8 (1957):223.

19. On the statement of al-Rimawi, see "Ba'th Party Statement on Eisenhower's Middle East Policy," report dated January 10, 1957, ISA, File 443-3; A. Sela, "Mifleget ha-ba'th," in "Ha-Miflagot ha-politiyot ba-Gada ha-Ma'aravit," ed. Amnon Cohen, mimeographed (Institute of Asian and African Studies, The Hebrew University of Jerusalem, 1972), p. 174.

to a friend. . . . These warnings are a service that Russia is rendering to the world. Furthermore, this is proof that the Soviet Union honors high principles and moral values incomparably more than the Western world."[20]

The change in the government's attitude toward the Communist countries was accompanied by a change in attitude toward the Jordanian Communist party. On assuming office, the Nabulsi cabinet released three imprisoned party leaders, Fu'ad Nassar, 'Abd al-Rahman Shuqayr, and Muslim Basisu. The Communist party organ, *al-Jabha al-Wataniyya* (The National Front), was legally allowed to appear, and Communist party statements began to be published in Jordanian newspapers. Moreover, Nabulsi's cabinet included 'Abd al-Qadir al-Salih of the National Front, who was known for his Communist leanings.[21]

Termination of the Anglo-Jordanian military treaty, rejection of the Eisenhower Doctrine, and rapprochement with the Communist countries all demonstrated the opposition parties' use of Amman's concession policy to advance their political interests through support and ideological inspiration from abroad, particularly from Egypt. The opposition parties tended to subordinate national Jordanian considerations on domestic and foreign policy issues to the interests of Cairo. Nabulsi consulted the Egyptian ambassador in Jordan on political matters, and it is even thought in some quarters that he consulted with President Nasir himself.[22]

Amman's concession policy and the opposition's exploitation of political resources outside the kingdom reduced the hostility of the opposition parties toward Amman and concomitantly strengthened the pattern of conditional legitimacy. This pattern existed as long as Amman's policy could be interpreted by the opposition as coinciding with its political goals and with those of the regimes in Syria and Egypt. Evidence of this attitude could be found among al-Ba'th, al-Qawmiyyun, and even among the Communists.

Notwithstanding the Ba'th's goals of "Unity, Freedom, and

20. *Filastin,* November 7, 1956.
21. *HMH* 8 (1957):146.
22. See, for instance, Aqil Abidi, *Jordan: A Political Study, 1948–1957* (New York: Asia Publishing House, 1965), p. 155.

Socialism" in a democratic republic, the party was willing to collaborate with the Jordanian monarchy during this period. It welcomed
the government's dismissal of General Glubb and called for the
termination of the treaty with Britain.[23] Jordan's cooperation with
Syria and Egypt was also welcomed as a positive step toward Arab
unity. This did not stop the Ba'th in later years, however, from
calling King Hussein "imperialism's foster child," who cooperated
with the Saudi Arabian king in order to hamper socialist-oriented
political movements in the Arab world.[24]

Al-Qawmiyyun, which was far from sympathetic to the regime,
also muted its hostility in these years. It responded enthusiastically
to the government's announcement that it would not accede to the
Baghdad Pact and expressed its hope for Arab unity.[25] The Communists also supported the king's positive attitude toward the
Nabulsi government and announced its readiness to support any
government that adopted a "national, independent, and democratic" policy even if it did not serve in the cabinet.[26] This support
reflected the party's temporary acceptance of the Jordanian political
system as long as the regime's actions were compatible with the
party's interests—namely recognition of the party's legality and
rapprochement with the Eastern bloc.

The "Palestinian Entity"

The Syrian-Egyptian split in September 1961, after three years
of unity as the United Arab Republic, and the failure of the at-

23. See the joint Ba'th-National Socialist memorandum calling for renunciation of the treaty and Jordan's accession to the "triple alliance"; *Filastin,*
June 19, 1956.

24. See, for instance, "To the Arab Vanguard in Jordan," Ba'th party poster
dated November 11, 1962, ISA, File 707–3; Sela, "Mifleget ha-ba'th," p. 164.

25. In a document dated July 16, 1956, entitled "No Borders and No
Separate Entities," al-Qawmiyyun wrote: "Today the hated walls between
Syria and Jordan will be removed, today the hated remnants of imperialism
will disappear from our land . . . and all the artificial dividers which tear apart
our homeland are brought down and a united Arab state arises." See G.
Broide, "Al-Qawmiyyun al-'arab," in "Ha-Miflagot ha-politiyot ba-Gada ha-
Ma'aravit," p. 222.

26. See *al-Difa',* October 22 and 23, 1956; Amnon Cohen, "Ha-Miflaga
ha-qomunistit," in "Ha-Miflagot ha-politiyot ba-Gada ha-Ma'aravit," p. 33.

tempts to establish a tripartite union of Syria, Egypt, and Iraq in 1963 reflected the difficulties involved in attaining Arab union.[27] These events had a profound impact on Jordanian domestic politics. The conflicts between the three Arab regimes, which opened the possibility for Amman to reach individual rapprochements with them, affected relations between Amman and the opposition parties in the West Bank.

Opposition on the West Bank decreased in 1963 owing to two main factors. First, the Jordanian Revolutionary Council moved from Damascus to Cairo after the split between Syria and Egypt, and the greater distance from the West Bank meant that it became less effective there. Second, there was a rapprochement between Jordan and Egypt in January 1963 that helped to moderate the sharp disagreements between the regime and the West Bank. Against this background Amman adopted a more liberal policy toward the West Bank in order to recreate the conditions for rapprochement and collaboration.

Wasfi al-Tall, a Jordanian from Irbid in the East Bank, who was perceived by the Palestinians at that time as a liberal politician, was appointed to head three cabinets during the 1960s.[28] Al-Tall's governments were noteworthy for the youth and professional background of their members. His first cabinet, which was appointed after the Syrian secession from the United Arab Republic, did not include a single minister who had served in a previous cabinet. In his later cabinets the foreign affairs portfolio was held successively by Palestinians Hazim Nusayba, Rafiq al-Husseini, and Amin Yunis al-Husseini, all from prominent families originally from Jerusalem. The Ministry of Economic Affairs was headed by Rashid al-Khatib of the National Socialist party, and the embassy of Jordan in Egypt was headed by Anwar al-Khatib. Despite the fact that these offices were usually powerless in comparison to portfolios like those of interior minister and prime minister, the appointments served to

27. On the failure of these attempts, see Malcolm H. Kerr, *The Arab Cold War,* 3rd ed. (New York: Oxford University Press, 1971), pp. 77–95.

28. In November 1971 al-Tall was assassinated in Cairo by members of the Palestinian Black September group for his role as Jordanian prime minister during the 1970 civil war in Jordan between Palestinian guerrilla organizations and the Jordanian army.

stress the Palestinian presence in the governing system and to make it seem more representative.

As part of his liberalization policy, King Hussein, by a decree of May 13, 1963, pardoned a large group of officers and civilians sentenced to long prison terms for antigovernment activity.[29] In 1965 some political exiles, including 'Abdallah al-Tall, 'Ali Abu Nuwar, and 'Ali al-Hiyari, were permitted to return to Jordan.[30]

From 1962 on, Amman also employed economic planning as a way of manifesting its liberal nondiscriminatory policy toward the West Bank. A national economic plan covered both the industrial and agricultural sectors, applying to projects in the West Bank as well as in the East Bank. As part of the program to develop water resources, Jordan signed an aid agreement with the United States for the Ghor Canal project to provide irrigation for 30,000 acres of land on both sides of the Jordan River.[31] There were also projects on both banks for light industry, tourism, health, and education. This policy was clearly an attempt to divert the revolutionary potential of the political opposition groups in the West Bank to economic activity and increase the regime's capacity to bargain with them.

In the civil service, the liberal policy of Amman gave rise to a series of reforms during the 1960s aimed at giving the West Bank population a sense of equality. A decentralization policy increasing the authority of local governors gave them broad power over administrative appointments within their areas and over the local population. Regulations giving the government the right to dismiss inefficient or corrupt officials and legislation in 1964 empowering the comptroller general to investigate the sources of income of public officials were other attempts to create the feeling of equal treatment for the two banks.

At the same time Amman reassessed its Palestinian policy. In the

29. On the release of 460 political prisoners in May 1963, see *al-Manar*, June 16, 1963.
30. See Eliezer Be'eri, *Army Officers in Arab Politics and Society* (New York: Praeger, 1970), p. 234.
31. See *Filastin*, January 27, 1962.

late 1950s and early 1960s, when the slogan "Palestinian entity" was created by Iraq and Egypt, Jordan consistently opposed it.[32] However, in January 1964, when the first Arab summit conference took place, Jordan decided to change its tactics, and the king joined in a motion recommending the establishment of a "Palestine Liberation Organization" (PLO) to permit the Palestinian people to play a part in all-Arab effort "in the liberation of their homeland and their self-determination."[33] In the letter the king sent to Wasfi al-Tall appointing him prime minister in February 1965, he wrote, "the government must support the Palestine Liberation Organization and cooperate closely with it in Jordan, the Arab homeland, and internationally."[34]

The roots of the Jordanian position emphasizing the resolution of the Palestine problem through a common all-Arab effort lay in a White Paper published by the Jordanian Foreign Ministry in July 1962:

> Jordan, the heir of Palestinian sorrow and hopes . . . feels the urgent call to inject new life into the Palestinian problem . . . and to move it from deadlock to movement . . . and from a passive to an active level. The government of Jordan feels that it is charged with a heavy and special responsibility in this work since it is the place in which . . . almost two-thirds of the

32. On the thirty-first session of the Arab League in Cairo in 1959, which decided, on Egyptian initiative, to discuss the issue of "the reorganization of the Palestinians and giving them an entity of their own," see *al-Ahram* (Cairo), April 6, 1959. The former chairman of the PLO, Ahmad al-Shuqayri, claimed that anyone who mentioned the term "Palestinian entity" in Jordan before 1964 was in danger. See Ahmad al-Shuqayri, *Min al-qimma ila al-hazima ma' al-muluk wa al-rua'sa'* [From the summit to the defeat with the kings and rulers] (Beirut: Dar al-'Awda, 1971), p. 69.

33. From the "Final Communiqué of the First Summit Conference," January 1964, in *Tokhnit ha-pe'ula ha-'aravit neged Yisra'el 1949–1967* [The Arab plan of action against Israel, 1949–1967], ed. Yehoshafat Harkabi, Part 2 (Jerusalem: Academon, 1972), p. 11.

34. *Al-Yawmiyyat al-filastiniyya, 1965* [The Palestine yearbook], ed. Habib Rafiq Mutlaq (Beirut: The Research Center, The Palestine Organization, 1966), p. 157.

Palestinian people, almost a million souls, live. . . . it also believes that the burden of the Palestine problem is heavy and requires a consistent effort . . . and general agreement by all the Arab states. The first step in unifying the effort is, first and foremost, getting away from splitting it up. The government of Jordan sorrowfully notes that it does not see in the present Arab political reality, particularly at the level of those in charge, any manifestations of realistic evaluation of this axiom.[35]

During the 1960s the Jordanian regime therefore, did not deny the need to deal with the Palestine problem, but it laid down strict conditions about how this might be done.

The revival of interest in a "Palestinian entity" in the early 1960s centered on an attempt to stress the dominant role of the Palestinians themselves in solving Palestine's problems, without neglecting the sensitivity of the issue among the Arab states or denying the inter-Arab connection. Ahmad al-Shuqayri, who became chairman of the executive committee of the PLO in the years 1964–68, demanded permission to organize the Palestinians politically in a Palestine Liberation Organization and militarily in a Palestine Liberation Army that would join in the all-Arab effort to liberate their homeland.[36] Al-Shuqayri's view was expressed in the Palestine National Charter of 1964 and the Constitution of the Palestine Liberation Organization. According to the charter "Palestine is an Arab homeland bound by the ties of Arab Nationalism to the other Arab countries which, together with Palestine, constitute the greater homeland."[37] Referring to the Palestine Liberation Organization, the charter states: "For the realization of the goals of the charter and its principles, the Palestine Liberation Organization shall per-

35. See al-Mamlaka al-urduniyya al-hashimyya, wizarat al-kharijiyya, [The Hashemite Kingdom of Jordan, Foreign Ministry], *Al-Urdun wa-al qadiyya al-filastiniyya wa-al 'ulaqat al-'arabiyya* [Jordan, the Palestine problem and Arab ties], as cited in *Tokhnit ha-pe'ula ha-'aravit,* part 2, pp. 63–64.

36. See the discussion on this point in al-Shuqayri, *Min al-qimma ila al-hazima,* p. 137.

37. See "The Palestinian National Charter of 1964," in *The Arab-Israeli Conflict,* ed. John Norton Moore, vol. 3, *Documents* (New Jersey: Princeton University Press, 1974), article 1, p. 700.

form its complete role in the liberation of Palestine, in accordance with the constitution of this organization." Yet it states explicitly that "this organization shall not exercise any territorial sovereignty over the West Bank [region] of the Hashemite Kingdom of Jordan, the Gaza strip, or the Himmah area. Its activities, in the liberational, organizational, political, and financial fields, shall be on the national-popular level."[38]

The PLO was careful not to interfere in the internal affairs of the Arab states and in their ideological dissensions, expressing its military ambitions by proclaiming that "special Palestinian units will be formed in accordance with military needs and plans decided upon by the Joint Arab Command, and with the agreement and cooperation of the Arab states concerned."[39]

Moreover, in order to head off conflicts liable to break out between the PLO and the Arab countries, particularly Jordan, Ahmad al-Shuqayri initiated a ten-article declaration which stated:

> the personality of the PLO stems from the conscience of the Palestinian people, and it will not interfere in any way in the internal affairs of Jordan, or of any other state. . . . [Furthermore] the organization undertakes a constant commitment to keep its distance from Arab dissensions. . . . Jordan is the homeland of the organization, and the people of Jordan are the people of the organization, and the organization takes care to cooperate to the maximum with the Jordanian government in the context of the objective of liberation.

38. Ibid., articles 23, 24, pp. 703, 704.

39. According to "The Constitution of the Palestine Liberation Organization, 1964," article 22 in *Tokhnit ha-pe'ula ha-'aravit*, part 2, p. 37. This article was changed in the 1968 version of the Constitution to: "The Palestine Liberation Organization shall form an army of Palestinians, to be known as the Palestine Liberation Army, with an independent command which shall operate under the supervision of the Executive Committee, and carry out its instructions and decisions, both general and particular. Its national duty is to become the vanguard in the battle for the liberation of Palestine." See "Constitution of the Palestine Liberation Organization," in *International Documents on Palestine 1968*, ed. Zuhair Diyab (Beirut: The Institute for Palestine Studies, 1971), p. 398.

According to another article of the declaration, the Jordanian government and the organization are two independent bodies:

> the first on the official level and the second on the popular level and they are like two lungs in one body. Just as in Israel, the Jewish Agency and the government work side by side with no contradiction or clash [between them] . . . so the Jordanian government and the organization have a great national goal—to create an atmosphere of brotherhood for faithful cooperation.[40]

40. *Al-Watha'iq al-filastiniyya al-'arabiyya li-'am 1965* [Palestinian Arab documents for the year 1965] (Beirut: The Institute for Palestine Studies, 1966), pp. 414–15. A PLO memorandum written in preparation for discussions between the representatives of the organization and the Jordanian government in February 1965 expressed similar views:

1. The Organization is determined not to assume any sovereignty whatsoever on either side of the Jordan or to establish a Palestinian government in the homeland or in exile.
2. The Organization's policy is not directed at tearing the West Bank apart from the East Bank. The Organization concentrates all its national efforts on the liberation of the stolen part of Palestine. And it leaves it to the Palestinian people to decide their destiny after liberation.
3. The Organization does not differentiate between the citizens of Jordan and considers them equal in rights and duties. . . . Consequently, all the military and civilian activities of the Organization are open to all citizens of Jordan without discrimination.
4. The Organization does not interfere in the internal affairs of Jordan and is not opposed to the Jordanian entity at all.
5. The Organization is proud of the Jordanian army, of its commanders, officers, and soldiers of all units and forces, considers it a Palestinian army and sees in it great hope for liberation. . . .
6. The demands of the Organization stem from the highest Arab interest, which calls for the preparation of the Palestinian people for carrying out its historic task in liberating its homeland. . . .
7. The popular activity of the Organization in Jordan does not exclude the official activity of Jordan. Indeed, they support and complement each other.
8. The Organization has an independent character shaped by the character of the Palestinian people. The Organization cooperates with all Arab states and does not follow any one of them.

See Maktab munazzamat al-tahrir al-filastiniyya fi al-jumhuriyya al-'arabiyya al-muttahida [The Palestinian Liberation Organization Office in the UAR],

These formulations, however, could not cover up the potential conflict inherent in the contrasting views each side had on the solution of the Palestinian problem. Though the PLO's demands emphasized extraterritorial aspirations, Jordan saw its aims as embodying a wish to create a second military and political system in Jordan threatening its sovereignty. Shuqayri's attempts to distinguish between the official level in Jordan and the popular level were no help in narrowing the differences between them.

Nonetheless, Jordan desired to coexist with the West Bank by avoiding ideological conflict with the Palestinians over the most sensitive issue. That desire was reflected in its policy to pass off the debate with the supporters of the "Palestinian entity" simply as a dispute not over the ultimate goal of liberation of Palestine but over the tactics that would serve this goal best. Paradoxically, the emphasis in the West Bank from the early 1960s on its Palestinian consciousness facilitated Amman's policy. The emergence of this consciousness allowed Amman to try to mute the short-run differences between itself and the West Bank by emphasizing mutual goals with the Palestinians for the long run. This was in contrast to earlier periods, when the West Bank public attributed greater importance to the Nasirist and Ba'thist political option, which made it difficult for Amman to draw the distinction between tactics and goals.

Even in the years 1965-67, when the quarrel between Amman and the PLO culminated in the use of force against the organization, Amman tried to advance its particular interest under the guise of debate with the PLO over tactics, not goals. The PLO argued that the Jordanian government was sowing discord in Jordan and the Arab world as a whole, while Jordan maintained that a solution required pan-Arab efforts. "We do not recognize" proclaimed King Hussein, "the usefulness . . . of an element or organizations, or of improvised activity . . . which deviates from the guidelines of the Joint Arab Command and united Arab planning . . . since it is liable

---

Nashrat howl mofawadat munazzamat al-tahrir al-filastiniyya ma' hukumat al-Urdun [Statement on PLO discussions with the Jordanian government] (Cairo, 1966).

to make Arab planning difficult . . . and provide our enemies with an opportunity to attack."[41]

Hussein made a similar point, in more detail, in his letter to President Nasir in October 1965 explaining his position in the conflict with the PLO:

> The argument that al-Shuqayri uses . . . is that Jordan hampers the organization's activity and does not give it freedom of action. Freedom of action, in his view and as has become manifestly clear, is meant to tear the Palestinian Jordanian citizen to the west of the river away from his brothers, the Palestinian Jordanian citizen to the east, to revive an antagonism which disappeared and was buried, to rouse the civil war from its sleep, to split the unity of the people and the army . . . and to hurt the effort aimed at further military concentration and preparation, in accordance with the decisions of the summit conference and the orders of the Joint Arab Command.[42]

Paradoxically, the conclusion Amman drew from its distinction between the strategic-fundamental level and the tactic-operational one, coincided with the view of radical parties like the Ba'th and al-Qawmiyyun, which also supported a pan-Arab approach to the issue. Amman, however, exploited the pan-Arab argument to stifle independent action by the Palestinian public in order to preserve the status quo. The Palestinian radicals used the same argument to change the status quo through the realization of a pan-Arab vision rather than through separate Palestinian efforts.[43]

---

41. See *al-Watha'iq, 1965*, document 192, p. 546.

42. *Al-Watha'iq, 1966*, document 255, p. 569. This perception is also the basis of Wasfi al-Tall's declaration that Ahmad al-Shuqayri's ambition to establish parallel governmental machinery in Jordan, as an organizational framework for the Palestinian population there, would weaken Jordan and undermine the common Arab endeavors in Palestine. Al-Tall claimed that al-Shuqayri's demands were motivated by the love of "dominion and authority, and whoever . . . knows al-Shuqayri knows that this is his eternal weak point." Ibid., document 125, p. 302.

43. On al-Qawmiyyun's attitude toward the "Palestinian entity," for instance, see Walid al-Qamhawi, *Al-Nakba wa-al bina' fi-al watan al-'arabi* [Disaster

The Ba'th and al-Qawmiyyun therefore rejected the call for the First Palestine Congress in May 1964, which was held in Jerusalem. The Ba'th was also opposed to the establishment of the PLO and on the eve of the congress wanted to stage demonstrations calling for its elimination.[44] Al-Qawmiyyun circulated a warning about the absence of a "revolutionary" element in the congress's talks: "Giving al-Shuqayri a free hand in everything," it argued, "far from creating effective popular control raises a possibility of a return to the wretched manner in which the Arab Higher Committee conducted the struggle of the Palestinian people before the disaster."[45]

However, the differences between the Ba'th, al-Qawmiyyun, and the PLO narrowed after 1966, when Amman began severely suppressing them all.[46] They developed a common interest in "liberating" Jordan from Hashemite rule as a necessary condition for the liberation of Palestine. They also examined the possibility of establishing a united movement, but nothing came of that.

Despite the rift between the Palestinian opposition and the regime, the latter continued to try to maintain coexistence through the conditional legitimacy pattern by advocating a pan-Arab solution to the Palestine problem while decrying the opposition's tactics. Furthermore, the regime's position on the Palestinian issue found support in the resolutions of the third Arab summit conference, which met in Casablanca in September 1965 and rejected al-Shuqayri's demands for "freedom of action for the popular

---

and reconstruction in the Arab homeland] 2nd ed., vol. 2 (Beirut: Dar al-'ilm lil-malayin, 1962), pp. 421–23; Broide, "Al-Qawmiyyun al-'arab," pp. 248–49.

44. For details on these activities, see report dated December 2, 1964, ISA, File 653–7.

45. See "Clarifications about the Palestine National Congress," poster of June 1964, ISA, File 498–4. For similar arguments see *al-Watha'iq, 1965,* document 165, pp. 476–78.

46. On the activity of the Jordanian government against the opposition see, for instance, *al-Yawmiyyat, 1966,* p. 131; on Amman's withdrawal of its recognition of the PLO in January 1967, see *al-Yawmiyyat, 1968,* p. 342.

organization of the Palestinians and . . . direct general elections to the Palestine National Council."[47]

CONDITIONAL LEGITIMACY AS A
COMPROMISING ELEMENT

The pattern of growing conditional legitimacy that characterized the 1950s and 1960s can be seen as a substitute for full Palestine loyalty to the regime in Amman and indicates recognition that the conflict with Jordan was essentially temporary. It provided an opportunity for both parties to negotiate conflictual pressures and cooperative interests and was the basis for the coexistence of the two banks.

From the Palestinian point of view, it was a way for the West Bank to maintain political affiliation with the kingdom without abandoning its ultimate objectives. This affiliation was based less on voluntary acceptance of Jordan's political symbols and beliefs than on the economic and geopolitical constraints in the West Bank after annexation.

From Amman's standpoint, although full legitimacy would have been much preferred, the flexible political arrangements were acceptable because of the delicate balance between the two banks and because of intervention of radical Arab regimes in Jordanian domestic politics after the mid-1950s. Amman's acceptance of conditional legitimacy as an expression of the Palestinian attitude toward the regime allowed it to continue viewing the population of the West Bank as an integral part of the Jordanian political system.

Amman accepted conditional legitimacy rather than full legitimacy because the Palestinians' use of Nasirist and Ba'thist versions of pan-Arabism provided the regime with a handle to manipulate them. Amman could use the same pan-Arab arguments to justify cooperating with some of the radical Arab regimes against the Palestinian interpretation of the ultimate goal, that is, the liberation of Palestine. By expressing its political position in pan-Arab terms, Jordan not only lessened the risk of immediate rejection of its

47. See "Final Communiqué of the Third Summit Conference," September 1965, article 7, in *Tokhnit ha-pe'ula ha-'aravit,* ed. Yehoshafat Harkabi, p. 17.

policy by the West Bank but also stressed that the differences between them had narrowed. Paradoxically, then, the source of Palestinian bargaining power through pan-Arabism was also a source of vulnerability. Conditional legitimacy not only served Palestinian interests but was also exploited by the regime to manipulate those interests.

4

Palestinian Identity
and the Struggle over Meaning

The annexation of the West Bank by Jordan and conditional acceptance by the Palestinians of Jordanian authority made it more difficult for the Palestinians to define their political identity.[1] Pan-Arab ideologies, which all shared an aspiration for Arab unity, appealed to the Ba'thists and supporters of President Nasir on the West Bank. Concomitantly pan-Islamic ideologies served as an option for the Muslim Brotherhood and the Tahrir party. As a result of the conflict between the two banks and the partial estrangement of the Jordanian establishment from the Palestinian population, however, the awareness of a specific identity as Palestinians grew stronger. Alongside these three collective identities— pan-Arab, pan-Islamic, and Palestinian—there also existed the West Bank affiliation to Jordan. This Jordanian "identity," however, was not sustained by the same political symbols and set of beliefs that engendered devotion to the pan-Arab and Palestinian identities. It materialized mostly in participation in the political life of Jordan and in dependence on resources allocated by the regime in Amman. These four ways of defining collective identity—pan-Arab, pan-Islamic, Palestinian, and Jordanian—played a central role in shaping West Bank political behavior toward Amman and the rest of the

1. Despite the wide usage of the term *identity,* there is no uniform definition of it. For our purposes we shall define identity, as Miller does, as a set of perceptions and attitudes which the individual or group holds about itself; see Daniel R. Miller, "The Study of Social Relationships: Situation, Identity, and Social Interaction," in *Psychology: A Study of a Science,* ed. S. Koch, vol. 5 (New York: McGraw-Hill, 1963), pp. 670, 673.

74

Arab world. It is here one should look to grasp how the Palestinians' desire to realize their political identity through an independent entity was balanced for many years by the ability to redefine Palestinianism according to Jordanian, pan-Arab, and pan-Islamic identities.

The different political groups in the West Bank related in different ways to each of the optional identities. Those Palestinians who joined the Jordanian establishment as senior officials and those who ran for seats in the House of Representatives tended to stress the Jordanian and sometimes the pan-Arab identities. Opponents of the Jordanian monarchy, particularly members and supporters of opposition parties, emphasized the Palestinian and pan-Arab or pan-Islamic identities. Sometimes individual figures changed their evaluation of the four potential identities. Political identity was a critical resource in the bargaining process among the political groups in the West Bank. The identity of the Palestinians was influenced by the Jordanian policy of binding individuals to its side by granting them political favors as well as by larger policy shifts in other Arab countries.

SHIFTING EMPHASES IN WEST BANK POLITICAL IDENTITY

The West Bank's simultaneous bond to the Palestinian and Jordanian "official" identities in the first years after annexation had a great impact on Amman–West Bank relations. West Bank political leaders confronted the conflict between resigning themselves to being part of Jordan and working to fulfill their political goal of a separate Palestinian identity. During the years 1949–54 the Palestinians received little support from outside Jordan. While some Arab governments criticized King 'Abdallah's policies toward Britain, Israel, and the refugees, they did not try to exploit their links with Amman's opposition in the West Bank in order to change Jordanian policies. The limited influence of the Arab regimes restricted the impact of pan-Arab consciousness in the West Bank. The main tension, then, was between the West Bank's sense of being Palestinian and its sense of being Jordanian.

Pan-Arabism achieved greater importance only after the mid-

1950s. The impact of the Nasirist and Ba'thist version of pan-Arabism on political behavior in the West Bank was reflected in the emphasis of political parties on political problems of all-Arab significance rather than on local Jordanian problems. Furthermore, even Jordanian domestic problems were not judged solely in their Jordanian context but according to broader, usually pan-Arab criteria. These considerations were apparently part of an attempt by the Palestinians to use the pan-Arab option as a means of giving political substance to their Palestinian identity. Yet from the mid-1950s to the early 1960s pan-Arabism served to obscure the autonomy of the Palestinian identity. The pan-Arab aspect of the West Bankers' consciousness grew at the expense of the Palestinian aspect. At that time the tendency of political groups in the West Bank to envisage their political existence in pan-Arab terms was shared also by some nationalist elements in the East Bank. They saw in the pan-Arab option a solution to Jordan's political insecurity. A political union between Jordan and the United Arab Republic as a step toward unity of the Arab world became the main issue in the political life of the opposition to Amman on both banks.

As we have seen, the opposition's sensitivity to pan-Arab sentiments influenced its attitudes toward the Baghdad Pact, the dismissal of General Glubb, and relations with the radical Arab regimes. This is a striking contrast to the previous period of 1949 to 1954 when the opposition tended to emphasize Palestinian and Jordanian identities—not the pan-Arab identity. The focus after the mid-1950s on pan-Arab options was not simply an attempt by the West Bank Arabs to realize the Palestinian dream through pan-Arab means but was also an effort to resolve an ambiguous situation by advocating a single collective identity.

In the early 1960s there was a reversal of the pan-Arab trend, as the Palestinian identity became an increasingly important factor in political behavior in the West Bank, casting a shadow on the Jordanian as well as the pan-Arab option. This trend was reflected in the tension that arose between Amman and opposing groups in the West Bank over the issue of the Palestinian entity. In chapter 3, we saw that the idea of the entity was revived in the late 1950s, largely at President Nasir's initiative. It marked the beginning of what can be called "re-Palestinization" of the political mood in the West Bank. While the United Arab Republic tended to give a political interpretation to the term "Palestinian entity" and Iraq adopted a military one, the Jordanian regime at that time firmly opposed the entire approach of a "Palestinian entity."[2] Amman's hostility to the idea of a Palestinian nation, its monopoly over military and economic power, and the split among the radical Arab regimes during the 1960s made it difficult for the West Bank supporters of the "Palestinian entity" to give real substance to their Palestinian identity. At that time the Palestinian opposition did not perceive as a realistic option widening the rift between itself and Amman to a point of no return. This served to temper West Bank enthusiasm during the 1960s for a Palestinian entity. Some Palestinian political leaders tried to gloss over contradictions in their relations with Amman by resorting to complex and sometimes ambiguous formulas in defining their political goals. Even Ahmad al-Shuqayri, chairman of the Palestine Liberation Organization (PLO) in the mid-1960s, disavowed any ambition of territorial sovereignty over the West Bank, the Gaza strip, or the Syrian-controlled al-Hamma area.

In sum, during the years of Jordanian rule in the West Bank, except during the period 1957 to 1961, the major West Bank political groups attempted to balance the various definitions of their political identity without leaning too heavily on any one. The situation they were in for so long, which prevented them from realizing their desires independently of other Arab countries, increased their need to maintain all four—partially conflicting, sometimes complementary—conceptions of their collective identity.

"FLOATING IDENTITY" AND THE
STRUGGLE OVER UNITY

The ability of the West Bank to preserve coexistence with Amman for a protracted period, in spite of the claims of four political identities, was made possible by a pattern of allegiance that can be

2. For more details see Elizer Be'eri, "Mashma'uto shel munah ha-yeshut ha-palestinit" [The meaning of the term Palestinian entity] mimeographed, (n.p., n.d.).

called "floating identity." Each political group in the West Bank was able to search for an alternative definition of the boundaries of the Palestinian collectivity in Jordan without unequivocally committing itself to the central symbols and political beliefs of any existing Arab regime.

Floating identity stimulated greater concern with social and political issues of pan-Arab or pan-Islamic significance, especially Arab and Muslim unity and the struggle against non-Arab or non-Muslim forces, than with issues of local Jordanian interest. Attitudes and programs of political groups became more messianic and utopian in tone. Proposals for attaining Islam's or the Arabs' ultimate objectives of unity by reforming the individual Arab and purifying his soul captured attention, while the need to deal with pressing day-to-day economic and social issues got very low priority. Emphasis on the ultimate goals shared by all Arab states and avoidance of practical suggestions for realizing them helped to reduce tension between the four foci of identity, although floating identity did not eliminate conflict completely. To be sure, there was more to their political world view than just prescriptions for unification; the relationship of the individual and the state, for example, was also an important issue. Unity, however, was the most decisive determinant in defining their collective identity and realizing their political desires.

The Ba'th and al-Qawmiyyun al-'arab: Political Identity through Arab Unity

The Ba'th and al-Qawmiyyun in the West Bank attributed the Arabs' failures and successes to the extent to which unity was realized. According to the Ba'th, unity was "a total perception of the life of the national Arab in every place."[3] Realization of the ideal did not mean merely the establishment of a united political framework but also a long process of reform and social renewal. This

---

3. 'Abdallah Na'was in *Filastin,* October 6, 1953; A. Sela, "Mifleget ha-ba'th" in "Ha-Miflagot ha-politiyot ba-Gada ha-Ma'aravit," ed. Amnon Cohen, mimeographed (Institute of Asian and African Studies, The Hebrew University of Jerusalem, 1972), p. 155.

renewal was considered by al-Qawmiyyun "the take-off point for growth, creativity, and a free and honorable life."[4]

The principle of Arab unity took priority over other principles in the platforms of both parties. Freedom and socialism, for instance, were viewed as means of realizing unity rather than as ends in themselves. Thus the Ba'th party maintained that national liberation was a goal whose realization was necessary if unity was to be achieved. Socialism at the same time would help the Arab nation to "bind its parts together tightly."[5]

Both parties saw the disunity of the Arab peoples as the main reason for their weakness. 'Abdallah Na'was, a Ba'th leader in the West Bank, argued that disunity led the Arab leaders to deal "with each area and its problems separately. The diagnosis of problems also varies from region to region and the disease of division grows worse."[6] For both parties the solution of the Palestine problem was dependent on the achievement of Arab unity. "The full and true solution of the problem," according to Na'was, "will be realized by means of unity."[7] "Unity," proclaimed al-Qawmiyyun, "will bring . . . power that will remove Jewish existence in the heart of our nation and restore our beloved Palestine to us."[8]

The realization of Arab unity required, according to both parties, far-reaching reforms in Arab leadership, in individual personality, and in Arab society. Though the political leadership in every Arab country expressed support for Arab unity, the Ba'th and al-Qawmiyyun maintained that most of the Arab leaders preferred the existing political frameworks to full Arab unity.[9]

4. From al-Qawmiyyun leaflet, "No Borders and No Separate Entities," of June 16, 1956; G. Broide, "Al-Qawmiyyun al-'arab," in "Ha-Miflagot ha-politiyot ba-Gada ha-Ma'aravit," p. 217.

5. See Dustur hizb al-ba'th al-'arabi al-ishtiraki [The Constitution of the socialist Arab Ba'th party], General Principles, article 4, ISA, File 690; Sela, "Mifleget ha-ba'th," p. 177.

6. 'Abdallah Na'was in *Filastin,* October 6, 1953.

7. 'Abdallah Na'was in *Al-Difa',* July 12, 1953.

8. Al-Qawmiyyun leaflet, "Arab Assistance—Victory of the People's Will," of January 1957; Broide, "Al-Qawmiyyun al-'arab," p. 218.

9. On this argument see ISA, File 623–11.

Al-Qawmiyyun also emphasized the need to mobilize the Arab people in the struggle for unity. The lack of a popular base, according to Al-Qawmiyyun, brought about the failure of the Syrian-Egyptian union in 1961.[10] Similarly the Ba'th argued that the union had failed because the public in Syria and Egypt was prevented from playing an active role through "its popular organizations."[11] Changes in the Arab personality were a condition for the realization of Arab unity, according to al-Qawmiyyun, and required increasing the capacity of the individual to challenge his weaknesses by adopting new patterns of behavior and thinking. The Arab individual is a fatalist, they argued; "he evades assuming responsibility, is lost in fantasies, and lives in hope of miracles. . . . he tends [to be] emotional, [and this] leads to emotional outbursts."[12]

In order to free individuals from this way of thinking, al-Qawmiyyun demanded that each Arab try to shake off his old heritage. Then he would become a person "who faces reality bravely and with determination . . . a man who makes his own destiny and does not give up. . . . [He will become] a realistic person who weighs matters on scales uninfluenced by emotion."[13]

However, the attainment of unity depended not only on changes in leadership, in popular action, and in the characteristics of the individual Arab but also on guidance by a revolutionary vanguard. The Ba'th set itself the task of being the nation's vanguard by uniting "the other mass popular organizations such as the workers' unions, youth and student organizations, cooperatives, and consumers' organizations."[14] Al-Qawmiyyun, on the other hand, set forth the characteristics considered necessary in a member of the vanguard. The member had to be willing to improve the present situation and confident of his ability to do so. He also had to be

10. See a statement by al-Qawmiyyun concerning the Arab unification plan, ISA, File 680–11; Broide, "Al-Qawmiyyun al-'arab," p. 227.

11. Al-Ba'th statement in *al-Hayat* (Beirut), May 26, 1962.

12. See *al-Wahda* of August 1962, ISA, File 623–11; Broide, "Al-Qawmiyyun al-'arab," p. 243.

13. Ibid.

14. See the Ba'th publication, "Comparison of Forms of Political Organization in Egypt, Syria, and Iraq after the Talks on the Tripartite Union," September 1963, ISA, File 441; Sela, "Mifleget ha-ba'th," p. 151.

capable of constant self-criticism to "purge his soul." Self-criticism "forbids him to lie," as Walid Qamhawi put it, even to himself. It forbids him to betray and forbids him to hate, even secretly, because hatred is deadly poison."[15]

Vanguard movements were to be established in every Arab state. They had to "be tightly bound to one another. . . . All will unite in the unity of the Arab vanguard movements that will carry the socialist Arab revolution through the homeland."[16] The realization of Arab unity was thus linked with a process of renewal embracing both the individual and society but ending in an indeterminate future. Moreover, by casting the solution in long-run terms, radical action in the present, which could accelerate tendencies to define unequivocally their political identity, could be avoided.

The perception of pan-Arabism in futuristic, total-unity terms increased the tendency among the Ba'th and al-Qawmiyyun to regard every Arab state as an integral part of the political framework to be established, even if its present behavior was contrary to their conception of unity. The Jordanian political system, in this respect, was viewed in terms not only of its current attitudes and behavior but also its participation in the united Arab state to be.

The tendency of the Ba'thists and al-Qawmiyyun to avoid as far as possible dealing with current issues of Jordanian concern provides further evidence of their concentration on political goals whose realization was reserved for the indefinite future. This can be seen in the low priority they gave to Jordan's economic and social problems despite the centrality of socialist ideas in a Ba'thist platform and in al-Qawmiyyun programs especially from the 1960s on. The Ba'th party platform stated, for example, that "economic wealth in the homeland is the property of the nation." Furthermore, it declared that "the present distribution of resources in the Arab homeland is unjust." The party considered it vital that steps were taken toward "the nationalization of the great natural resources, the major means of production, and the means of transportation."[17] According to al-Qawmiyyun, the social and political order should be based

15. Cited in Broide, "Al-Qawmiyyun al-'arab," p. 246.
16. Ibid., p. 247.
17. *Al-Dustur,* articles 26, 27, 29.

on the close cooperation of farmers, workers, and the educated as well as on the revolutionary political organizations charged with realizing socialism in the state of unity. Such a regime would strive to diminish the inequalities between the classes by transferring the means of production from private hands to "the hands of the masses" and to ensure the rights of the individual through "democratic, revolutionary, and representative institutions."[18]

The Ba'thists and their representatives in Parliament, however, took no practical steps to implement this policy and indeed paid minimal attention to it. On the rare occasions when they were discussed, economic issues were generally used as a way of making broader arguments about economic dependence on foreign forces and the need to build an economy based on Arab finances.[19]

Nor did the Ba'th concern itself too much with social issues, despite the high priority they received in the party platform. While it outlined a social regime to assure the worker sufficient income to satisfy his needs and a legal system to safeguard his rights and duties, one cannot point to a single concrete step it took to realize these aims. Of the host of Ba'thist publications, a very small number dealt with this issue, and the party leaders' initiatives on social affairs were marginal. A striking example of a publication in which social policy was in fact discussed was a memorandum that Na'was and al-Rimawi wrote in 1953 in which demands for legislation to workers from unemployment and from increases in their cost of living and to give them the right to organize were included.[20] The Ba'thists' interest decreased even further in later years when the political influence of the radical Arab regimes on relations between the two banks grew significantly.

The distinction between the all-Arab plane and the local Jordanian political plane reduced the possibility of a rift with Amman, but

18. Statement of al-Qawmiyyun, ISA, File 680–11.

19. On one of these rare occasions, see, for example, the memorandum of al-Rimawi and Na'was in September 1952 to Prime Minister Tawfiq Abu al-Huda about "Handing the Economy Through Action Planned to Cover a Number of Years," *Filastin*, September 23, 1952; Sela, "Mifleget ha-ba'th," pp. 144–46.

20. See *Filastin*, May 20, 1953.

when issues like freedom of speech and the right of political organization were considered by the Ba'th and al-Qawmiyyun as crucial
to their political survival the distinction became obscured. Both
parties conducted a political struggle for constitutional amendments
to democratize political life in Jordan. However, this reflected not
only their Arab consciousness but also their willingness to acquiesce
in their Jordanian "official" identity, at least in the short run.

The Muslim Brotherhood and the Tahrir Party:
Political Identity through Muslim Unity

Just as pan-Arabism was the core of the political world view of
the Ba'th and al-Qawmiyyun, so pan-Islamism became the major
element in the definition of political identity for the Muslim
Brotherhood and the Tahrir party. Their ultimate goal was to give
the future unified state a clear Muslim character that would pave
the way for an Islamic state. According to both the Muslim Brotherhood and al-Tahrir, Islam had not only a religious function but
a decisive role in defining the nature of the political and social order
as well.[21] Both parties therefore rejected any attempt to separate
religion from the state. Such a separation, they argued, was not
recognized by Islam but was the result of the imposition of Euro-
pean political views.[22]

The Muslim Brotherhood as well as al-Tahrir considered the
Islamic view of the nature of the state as synonymous with democ-
racy. The future Islamic state should be seen as the model of the
ideal state. "Islam has already been tested," argued al-Tahrir, "and
proven ideal. It suited every people and land it was brought to,
whereas imperialism created oppression and wars wherever it set
foot."[23]

21. On the idea that Islam has to shape the economy and society see, for
instance, Nizam al-ikhwan al-muslimun fi al-Khalil, 1949 [The Constitution of
the Muslim Brotherhood in Hebron], article 2, ISA, File 1274-6. See also
Simon, "Ha-Ahim ha-muslemim," in "Ha-Miflagot ha-politiyot ba-Gada ha-
Ma'aravit," p. 399.

22. *Al-Jihad,* December 21, 1954.

23. As cited in Simon and Landau, "Mifleget ha-shihrur," in "Ha-Miflagot
ha-politiyot ba-Gada ha-Ma'aravit," p. 595.

While the main objective was Muslim unity, Arab unity was regarded as a means to that end.[24] The principles of Arab unity were not, however, totally compatible with the Islamic world view and did not exclude the possibility of conflict between the pan-Arab interest, representing the political desires of the Arab countries, and the pan-Muslim interest, which embraced a wider population. A conflict between pan-Arab and pan-Muslim interest was apparent, for instance, in connection with the dispute between India and Pakistan over Kashmir. The Muslim Brotherhood criticized the support given by a number of Arab states to India against Muslim Pakistan. It also attacked the way in which some Arab states ignored the plight of Muslims in the USSR in order to avoid strains in their relations with Moscow.[25]

Al-Tahrir took an even harder line on Arab nationalism. It rejected such phrases as "the Arab nation," "national spirit," "sister states," and "national goals" as misleading and false. For al-Tahrir the term "nation" referred to a group bound together by an idea, while the ties among the Arabs were ties of blood; the Arabs were therefore a "people" (sh'ab), not a "nation" (umma). The concept of "sister states" was strongly criticized on the ground that it contravened Islamic theory, which opposed a multiplicity of states for Muslims.[26] From time to time sympathetic comments on Arab unity appeared in their publications, but when this occurred it was depicted as a way station on the road to Muslim unity.

The attitude of the Muslim Brotherhood and al-Tahrir toward Muslim unity also determined their position vis-à-vis the "imperialists." This term was usually used to designate the Western world and Israel, but sometimes it was extended to cover the Communist countries as well. Imperialism was considered the main cause of the backwardness of the Muslim world and of the Arab defeat in the 1948 war. It was seen to have a negative influence on Islamic culture, more so among Muslims in the Arab countries than in the Far East.[27] The impact of foreigners was felt in other areas of life

24. *Al-Jihad,* June 20, 1957; *HMH* 8 (1957):309.
25. Report dated February 20, 1958, ISA, File 718–40.
26. See Simon and Landau, "Mifleget ha-shihrur," p. 603.
27. See report dated April 20, 1955, ISA, File 718–40; Simon, "Ha-Ahim ha-muslemim," p. 358.

too. According to al-Tahrir, most of the Muslim world's economic and social difficulties were caused by the "imperialist" presence.[28]

By establishing Israel, al-Tahrir argued, the imperialists hoped to maintain their presence in the Muslim world, even if this required the continual expansion of the Jewish state.[29] The Muslim Brotherhood saw the development of the Negev desert and of Israeli shipping in the Red Sea as indicative of Israel's desire to take over contiguous Arab territories. Israel was even accused of plotting the conquest of Medina, one of the holy cities in Saudi Arabia, on the pretext that there had been a Jewish settlement there before the rise of Islam.[30] The party saw a danger that the Arabs would resign themselves to Israel's existence and give up the idea of liquidating Israel. This was the risk they saw in Jordan's efforts to solve the refugee problem through resettlement schemes and in the revival of the "Palestinian entity" idea, which they considered an attempt by the Arab states to shirk their responsibility for the Palestine problem.[31]

In addition to the role of foreign forces in weakening Islamic society, the Muslim Brotherhood and al-Tahrir maintained that fault also lay with internal social processes. The Muslim Brotherhood, for instance, saw the Jordanian decision to adopt a civil constitution from a French model as sapping the foundations of Islam. In their view, "it is the Islamic laws that prevent licentiousness and damage to morality, while the . . . imperialist laws prevent the unity of the Arabs and will lead to destruction and ruin."[32] Imprisonment without trial, which was practiced in Jordan, and the continued incarceration of prisoners even after they had served their full sentences was deemed by the Muslim Brotherhood to be contrary to Islamic law.

Al-Tahrir attacked Jordan's education policy for similar reasons.

28. See al-Tahrir's statement of September 15, 1955, in Simon and Landau, "Mifleget ha-shihrur," p. 594.

29. See, for instance, the Muslim Brotherhood's statement of July 25, 1953, ISA, File 982–16.

30. Report dated June 1, 1963, ISA, File 1/30 MM-40.

31. According to the "Commentary Page" of the Tahrir party dated July 18, 1961; Simon and Landau, "Mifleget ha-shihrur," p. 612.

32. See report dated May 23, 1964, ISA, File 370–24.

While some of the failings of the educational system were attributed
to the British policy of encouraging Western secular curricula at
the expense of religious instruction, others were seen as the fault
of the Jordanian authorities.[33] The manner in which the principles
of Islam were taught came in for criticism. The rot, the party
argued, had set in the Middle Ages, when the penetration of foreign
philosophies had led Muslims to neglect the study of Arabic and to
stray from the way of Islam. Since the nineteenth century, according to this argument, religious leaders had stressed the theoretical
aspects of religion rather than preached a way of life with clear-cut
patterns of behavior.[34]

Yet, as in the case of the Ba'th and al-Qawmiyyun, the goal of
unity of the Brotherhood and al-Tahrir produced future-oriented,
long-range, and ambiguous proposals rather than concrete ones for
the foreseeable future. The Brotherhood and al-Tahrir preached a
return to Islam and to behavior according to the tenets of the Qura'n
as the solution to the Palestine problem. "Never," argued the
Brotherhood in sermons, "will we be able to regain Palestine from
the robbers unless we put our trust in God."[35]

In this spirit the Tahrir party's leaders, who studied the methods
of the Prophet Muhammad, concluded that three phases would be
passed through before the Islamic state was established. The first
phase would come with the revelation of the messenger chosen by
God to spread the word of Islam. The second, the take-off phase,
would occur when the moral situation was right. These two phases
might, but need not, coincide. The advent of the third phase,
consolidation, would depend on how successful the preaching in
behalf of the Islamic state was.[36]

The vagueness and indeterminateness of the three phases did not
mean, however, that one should yield to apathy and sit back doing

33. Statement of October 30, 1955, ISA, File 718–40.

34. *Ara' hizb al-Tahrir* [Views of the Liberation party] (al-Quds, 1953),
pp. 5–10; Simon and Landau, "Mifleget ha-shihrur," p. 594.

35. Declaration of February 13, 1963, ISA, File MN 1/30 MM-21.

36. Ara', p. 52. See also the lecture by the Tahrir leader Da'ud Hamdan on
December 11, 1951, as summarized in Simon and Landau, "Mifleget ha-
shihrur," p. 595.

nothing. Quite the contrary; one must engage in a constant search among the Muslim communities for signs of redemption. Theoretically these signs might appear anywhere in the Muslim world, though al-Tahrir tended to concentrate on the Muslims of the Arab states, which it saw as the kernel around which it could crystallize support for its ideas.[37] During these stages, the party must work through "propaganda, such as the writing of books and leaflets, the publication of newspapers and periodicals, making speeches and lectures, holding meetings and ceremonies."[38]

Thus al-Tahrir, according to its publications, opposed the use of violence in order to attain its far-reaching political goals. The party leadership also opposed strikes and demonstrations as a means of undermining the regime in Amman. It saw Muhammad's method—prolonged educational campaigns—as a model for conducting the struggle. Al-Tahrir and the Brotherhood did not, however, reject war as a means of restoring Palestine to the Arabs. Indeed, "revenge on Israel is inevitable even if that means that only one Arab is left."[39] Such action, though, would require extensive preparation, and there did not seem to be any note of urgency in their calls for action. They recognized that Palestinian youth would need advanced military training in order to carry out successfully any mission against Israel.[40] A leader of the Muslim Brotherhood called for war

37. Some similarity can be discerned between this concept of political activity motivated by Islam and Max Weber's explanation in *The Protestant Ethic and the Spirit of Capitalism* of the motivation for capitalist economic activity in terms of the principles of Protestantism. In both cases, religion provides the impetus for activity which constitutes, in effect, the constant search for moral behavior of God's elect. In Weber's exploration, religion is seen to influence individual economic activity. In the Islamic case religion is perceived to inspire political solutions to be proposed to the public. Weber conducted a scientific investigation of the relationship between religious and economic factors in order to explain historical phenomena. For the Tahrir party, however, the relationship between religion and politics became a normative issue.

38. *Al-Sarih,* March 14, 1953.

39. From the Muslim Brotherhood's declaration of August 21, 1961, ISA, File 718–40.

40. See report dated December 24, 1962, ISA, File 718–40; Simon, "Ha-Ahim ha-muslemim," p. 383.

against Israel but stressed that he wished only to ensure "that the facts be in the heart of every Muslim and Arab so that he should not forget what happened to his brother."[41]

The fervent belief of the Muslim Brotherhood and al-Tahrir in ultimate political salvation through a Muslim state resulted in an inclination toward fundamental rather than practical solutions. For this reason, the pan-Islamists remained romantic reformers most of the time. Their political belief did not commit them to immediate action.

Both parties' marginal attention to domestic social and economic issues corresponded with their view that they were mainly concerned with reforming the Arab world by establishing an Islamic state at some point in the future. This does not mean that they ignored such issues completely. Referring to the Palestinian refugees, for instance, the Brotherhood complained that "There are people who live in a twenty-room mansion while there are people who sleep twenty to a room."[42] In a few isolated cases one can even point to a willingness on the part of both parties to raise social issues in Parliament and to conduct fund-raising campaigns for the poor. Such activity, however, was very restricted in comparison to the close attention paid to issues perceived to be of pan-Islamic significance, such as relations with Israel, the great powers, and other Arabs.

Al-Tahrir was even less interested than the Muslim Brotherhood in domestic issues. Even in its references to the future Islamic state it did not elaborate on social and economic matters. The party leaders merely declared that in the Islamic state poverty would be eradicated and the rights and obligations of workers and employers would be defined.[43]

Thus among the supporters of a pan-Islamic state the pattern of floating identity as an expression of equivocal commitment to any Arab state was made possible by the existence of two complementary factors. On the one hand, the pan-Islamic parties concentrated on general Islamic and Arab issues, their interest in

41. Ibid.
42. See declaration of December 2, 1964, ISA, File 370–24.
43. See Simon and Landau, "Mifleget ha-shihrur," p. 600.

the West Bank's domestic problems being marginal. On the other hand, the solutions to these general issues were said to require a protracted process with no immediate practical relevance. The pan-Islamic parties were therefore able to develop a cooperative political relationship with Amman on a day-to-day basis in spite of the possibility of conflict over the meaning of their cooperation.

The floating identity pattern did not cause the same difficulties for the pan-Islamic parties as it did for the Ba'thists and al-Qawmiyyun. The concept of the future united Arab state was based on a political frame associated partially with the radical Arab regimes in Syria, Egypt, and later Iraq. The fulfillment of the goals of the pan-Islamists, however, rested largely on a political frame still to be erected. Amman therefore did not perceive pan-Islamism as being as hostile as pan-Arabism. The possibility that the pan-Islamic al-Tahrir and Muslim Brotherhood could bridge the conflict with Amman on a practical level without giving up their ultimate objectives emerged as a realistic option.

Floating Identity and Conditions for Political Unity

The floating identity pattern of simultaneous attachment to more than one area of collective political inspiration was possible because pan-Arab and pan-Islamic political figures and movements in the West Bank tended to propose objectives that did not undermine the underlying political agreements. The pattern was affected by their assessment of their ability to accomplish more far-reaching political goals; the better the conditions for unity seemed to become the more they were inclined to forsake the pattern of floating identity for less equivocal, less ambiguous commitments. Whenever pan-Arab parties in the West Bank thought the probability of achieving the pan-Arab option was high the balanced coexistence among the four foci of identity—Palestinian, Jordanian, pan-Arab, and pan-Islamic—began to crumble. During the 1949–54 period, the conditions necessary for the West Bank to work for Arab unity did not exist. Their absence stemmed largely from the concept of Arab unity, in confederal terms, as cooperation among existing states rather than as the creation of a new integrative political framework. Arab unity then was not conceived of as having immediate importance. Palestinian and Jordanian identities could therefore coexist more easily in this period.

Opposition circles criticized Amman at that time for what they considered to be a dubious attitude toward Arab unity as a political principle. This criticism remained ineffective, however, as long as they received no external aid. In sum, once conditions seemed to permit real action, conflict between the political objectives of the West Bank and those of Amman would be exposed. So long as these conditions did not obtain, the exacerbation of Amman–West Bank relations could be avoided, and the West Bank political groupings could maintain their "floating identity."

After the mid-1950s, the large exposure of the West Bank public to the radical Arab regimes' versions of pan-Arabism created a sense that the conditions for realizing Arab unity were being fulfilled. This heightened the pan-Arab identity consciousness in the West Bank and made groups opposed to Jordanian rule more willing to tie their fate to Arab regimes outside Jordan. The formation of the United Arab Republic in 1958, which was perceived by the opposition on the West Bank as the first step toward Arab union, enhanced the Palestinian opposition's status to such an extent that extremist groups felt justified in resorting to violence against the Jordanian regime in order to realize the promise of unity. This was most striking in the 1957–61 period, when combined foreign and domestic efforts led to terrorist attacks throughout the kingdom and to assassination attempts against Jordanian political leaders.

With the failure during the 1960s of the radical Arab states' attempts for unity, and their ideal consequently seeming beyond reach, political groups in the West Bank reverted to coexistence among the four foci of identity. High Palestinian expectation of Arab unity was moderated. At the same time, cooperation between Amman and some of the radical Arab regimes increased. Jordan's rapprochement with Egypt, for instance, made it easier for the opposition parties in the West Bank to compromise with Amman. Even the resurrection of the Palestinian entity as a "hot" political issue in the early 1960s was not detrimental to coexistence among the four foci of identity as long as there seemed to be no effective way of giving the entity or the pan-Arab option real substance.

During most of the 1949–67 period, the pattern of floating identity contributed to flexible coexistence between the two banks. Floating identity can be considered a Palestinian attempt to maintain a balance among the alternative definitions of the Palestinian collective boundaries in a conflict situation. This attempt, however, was encouraged by the approach of Amman and the Palestinians to regard the conflict between them not as a situation of total opposition of interests but as an intermediate situation of prolonged tension, with a tendency to institutionalize the antagonism rather than to try to solve it through clear-cut decisions. In sum, floating identity allowed the Palestinian opposition to continue looking at its political destiny in Jordan as essentially transitory and at the possibility of change as involving developments beyond Jordan's borders.

5

Power and Ineffective Leadership

Although most of the political groups in the West Bank accepted Jordanian authority, tension between the two banks remained. The political struggle focused on the character of Amman's authority, the nature of its goals, and the scope of its activity. Both conditional legitimacy and floating identity helped ease tension by emphasizing durable though temporary political arrangements over final and permanent ones. Under these circumstances, each side tried to develop a system of relations in which resources it possessed were exchanged for more important ones. The regime in Amman tried to acquire political power over the Palestinians through its control of the decision-making machinery. The traditional local leaders in the West Bank tended to support Amman mainly in exchange for economic rewards. Opposition groups exposed to influence from other Arab states tended to accept coexistence with Amman, although implicitly and with reservations, in exchange for its recognition of some of their political beliefs and symbols.[1]

Whatever the exchange process between Amman and the West

1. One can look at power relations between the two banks and Amman's ability to exercise its authority over the population in the West Bank by using Lehman's three analytical categories of resources: "coercive-based," "normative-based," and "utilitarian-based." "Coercive resources" refers to the resources stemming from a regime's ability to exert its authority over the population located in its territory. "Normative-based resources" refer to the willingness of the population to identify with the accepted values and symbols of the political system. "Utilitarian-based resources" give the authorities a means of bargaining with the population, something to exchange for other resources. See E. W. Lehman, "Toward a Macro-Sociology of Power," *American Sociological Review,* 4 (1969): 454–56.

Bank was, both the traditional local elite that collaborated with Amman and the opposition groups that relied on Arab regimes were objects of surveillance, oppression, and manipulation by external forces rather than independent elements controlling their own resources. For most of the years between 1949 and 1967, Amman successfully prevented Palestinian rivals and supporters from forming or joining political bodies that would threaten Amman's control of the loci of power, so the Palestinians remained in an inferior political position. The power relations between the Palestinians and the Jordanians are illustrated by the regime's restrictions on political activity among the opposition parties and by its determination to keep the Palestinians from forming an all-West-Bank political leadership.

RESTRICTIONS ON THE OPPOSITION PARTIES' ACTIVITIES

The Palestinian opponents of the Jordanian regime were not particularly effective in their political actions. The regime's restrictions prevented them from effectively recruiting a core professional staff and from creating active party institutions. The disbanding of all political parties in Jordan in April 1957 made activity almost impossible.

The Communist party suffered most from government persecution. As early as 1951, leading party members, including the secretary-general, Fu'ad Nassar, were arrested in Amman in possession of the press used for party publications.[2] Legislative authority for the government's anticommunist campaign came with the enactment of the December 1953 Anticommunist Law, replacing the more lenient 1948 law. The regime's anticommunist campaign reached a peak in 1957, when King Hussein issued a bitter attack on communism, condemning it as an enemy of Arab nationalism.[3] The king attacked the party again in his speech to the people at

2. For more details see Amnon Cohen "The Jordanian Communist Party in the West Bank, 1950–1960," in *The USSR and the Middle East,* ed. Michael Confino and Shimon Shamir (New York: John Wiley and Sons, 1973), p. 427.
3. See King Hussein's letter to Sulayman al-Nabulsi in King Hussein, *Uneasy Lies the Head* (London: Heinemann, 1962), p. 133.

the end of April 1957, accusing it of having contacts with Israel and of wishing to make peace with the Jewish state.[4]

Statements like these laid the groundwork for the authorities' vigorous operations against the party. In May 1957 and early 1958, dozens of people were arrested in Jerusalem, Nablus, Jericho, and Bethlehem on suspicion of Communist activity. Jordanian authorities even revoked the immunity of two members of Parliament, Fa'iq Warad and Ya'qub Zia al-Din, who were then sentenced to long prison terms for membership in a Communist organization. The party's ranks were decimated, as many members fled from Jordan and others abandoned party activity either temporarily or permanently. The party was forced underground to protect itself from government suppression.[5]

Al-Qawmiyyun al-'arab, too, suffered from the actions of the Jordanian authorities. Suppression of the movement was stepped up from the mid-1950s on, when the party developed such close ties with the Syrian and Egyptian regimes that it was willing to smuggle arms into Jordan in order to overthrow the regime. Egyptian agents contacted party members to exchange information and to give instructions. The authorities responded by keeping a close watch on their activities and sometimes by arresting members. Among those arrested in 1958 for organizing strikes and demonstrations against the regime were Dr. Salah Ahmad al-'Anabtawi and Dr. Walid Qamhawi. Both were prominent figures in the party from Nablus.[6] The disbanding of all political parties at the end of April 1957 led al-Qawmiyyun to go underground.

The authorities' hostility to the Ba'th party became evident while the group was still being organized in the early 1950s. Its leaders in the West Bank, 'Abdallah al-Rimawi and 'Abdallah Na'was, were arrested, and restrictions were placed on the party's publications. Its

---

4. Amman Radio, April 25, 1957; Israel, *Summary of Arab Broadcasts*, no. 2257.

5. *Yearbook on International Communist Affairs, 1968* (Stanford, Calif.: Hoover Institution on War, Revolution, and Peace, 1969), p. 358.

6. Broide, "Al-Qawmiyyun al-'arab," in "Ha-Miflagot ha-politiyot ba-Gada ha-Ma'aravit," mimeographed (Institute of Asian and African Studies, The Hebrew University of Jerusalem, 1972), p. 185.

attempts between 1952 and 1955 to obtain a license as a political party were repeatedly rejected by the authorities on the ground that its principles were contrary to those of the Jordanian Constitution. After the mid-1950s teachers in high schools were fired for trying to spread Ba'thist ideas among their students.[7] At the same time Jordanian students in other Arab countries were kept under constant surveillance by the regime to keep them from being recruited to the party by the Syrian-Egyptian authorities. Teachers from Jordan who spent the summer at the universities of Damascus and Beirut were also watched to make sure that they had no contact with Ba'thists there.[8]

Al-Tahrir and the Muslim Brotherhood also came under close surveillance, although differences between the two parties created distinctions in Amman's policy toward them. While al-Tahrir aimed at establishing a united Muslim state on the ruins of the existing ones, the goal of the Muslim Brotherhood did not explicitly require the destruction of existing systems. Jordanian authorities consequently subjected members of al-Tahrir to a tough policy, while they treated the Brotherhood less severely.

Al-Tahrir ran into trouble very early on, when it applied for certification as a party. Its requests in late 1952 and early 1953 were rejected by the Minister of the Interior on the ground that its aims were contrary to the Constitution. Its founders, Sheikh Taqi al-Din al-Nabhani, Da'ud Hamdan, and Munir Shuqayr, were arrested for sedition. Government decrees forbade the employment of party members by state agencies, and civil servants in the Hebron district were warned not to join the party.[9] Consequently, al-Tahrir, like the Communist party, went underground. This led to a decline in the number of new members during the late 1950s and 1960s and cutbacks in the scope of party activity.

Although the regime was more tolerant of the Muslim Brother-

7. See report of February 25, 1956, ISA, File 443–3; Sela, "Mifleget ha-ba'th," in "Ha-Miflagot ha-politiyot ba-Gada ha-Ma'aravit," p. 97.

8. For an example of such surveillance, see report of June 26, 1960, ISA, File 390–11.

9. See *Filastin,* June 2, 1953; Simon and Landau, "Mifleget ha-Shihrur," in "Ha-Miflagot ha-politiyot ba-Gada ha-Ma'aravit," p. 415.

hood, there was some tension because of disagreements over government policy, especially on issues of religious significance. The government put the Brotherhood under surveillance and restraint insofar as it engaged in activity deemed detrimental to public security. Members of the Brotherhood were arrested in 1960 and 1965 after the party organized demonstrations against the official religious policy. The government claimed the arrests were necessary in order to keep members from making terrorist attacks on cinemas and places of amusement. Generally, however, differences between the government and the Brotherhood were not insurmountable, and sometimes they could even collaborate, especially against their common enemy, the Communists.[10]

Amman's surveillance of the parties effectively blocked attempts to recruit members from broad circles of the West Bank population. Most of the opposition parties thus concentrated their recruitment efforts on the educated groups of the population, particularly teachers and high school students. Students were thought to be a desirable element in the parties because of their "great political awareness and youthful susceptibility to political agitation and incitement which made them an important object of interest." The effort to recruit teachers also provided a way to spread new ideas to all parts of the kingdom. For "the practice of transferring teachers from place to place every few years . . . made them the ideal vehicle for the propagation of party ideology."[11]

The opposition's concentration on educated groups in the West Bank agrees with the views of analysts who see the intellectual elite charged with the main burden of revolutionary activity, taking on the role of the proletariat in the revolutionary process.[12] In the case of the West Bank this preference for intellectuals stemmed from practical as well as ideological considerations. The Palestinian

10. For more details see Cohen, "The Jordanian Communist Party," p. 420.

11. Cohen, "Political Parties in the West Bank under the Hashemite Regime," in *Palestinian Arab Politics,* ed. Moshe Ma'oz (Jerusalem: Jerusalem Academic Press, 1975), p. 36.

12. See, for instance, John H. Kautsky, ed., *Political Change in Underdeveloped Countries,* 4th ed. (New York: John Wiley and Sons, 1965), pp. 44–49.

general public perceived that opposition activity was considered by the regime to be deviant and often illegitimate. It stood little chance of success, so entering into party activity was not worthwhile. Among the educated groups, however, some saw an ideological satisfaction in opposition activity that made the risks and efforts worthwhile; merely trying to attain the ideologically determined goal added to one's self-esteem.

The recruitment policy of the Communist party focused on educated elements of the population only after a prolonged power struggle in the early 1950s between the two party leaders. Fu'ad Nassar and Ridwan al-Hilu. Nassar believed that efforts should be directed primarily toward the working class, where, he thought, the secret of future success lay, but al-Hilu tended to base the party's activity more on educated groups. Eventually al-Hilu's view prevailed, and the party tried to recruit members in the cities, principally among teachers and students. Teachers generally acted as centers of networks while students distributed leaflets, conducted agitational activity, and led street demonstrations. Physicians too, such as Ya'qub Zia al-Din, 'Abd al-Rahman Shuqayr, and 'Abd al-Hafiz al-Ashhab, played major roles in the party.[13] The party's concentration on educated groups was reflected in its small membership. In the early 1950s Jordanian sources estimated the party's membership at about 300, with 200 of this number in the West Bank. At the height of party activity, in 1956–57, the same sources estimated that there were no more than 1000 members.[14]

The Ba'th party's recruitment policy was similar. The party was especially active among teachers and students in high schools in Jerusalem, in Beit Hanina, and in the UNRWA school in the Bethlehem district.[15] The Ba'th, however, also tried to recruit members in the armed forces and the civil service. The party increased its

13. See Cohen, "Ha-Miflaga ha-comunistit," in "Ha-Miflagot ha-politiyot ba-Gada ha-Ma'aravit," pp. 27, 37–38.

14. See *Yearbook on International Communist Affairs, 1966,* p. 276, and Cohen, "The Jordanian Communist Party," p. 432.

15. On Ba'th activity in the Jerusalem area, see *Filastin,* October 19, 1957. On its activity in Beit Hanina and Bethlehem, see reports of January 3, 1956, ISA, File 496–1, and of April 14, 1956, File 443–4.

efforts to recruit military men and policemen in the late 1950s, when the armies of the Arab world began playing an increasingly important role in politics. These efforts were part of the preparations for the coup that the Ba'th planned for late 1959. The plan failed, however, and officers suspected of Ba'thist sympathies were discharged before they could threaten the regime's stability.[16] Despite its efforts, the Ba'th consisted in the main of a small core of activists not numbering more than a few hundred—between 500 and 700—in the late 1950s, all of whom were educated town and city dwellers.[17]

The other opposition parties developed along similar lines. The preventive acts of the regime against their activity forced al-Qawmiyyun, the Muslim Brotherhood, and al-Tahrir to devote most of their proselytizing energies to the recruitment of teachers and high school students, especially in Jerusalem, Nablus, and Ramallah. Nevertheless, these three parties did try more than the other opposition to extend their recruiting base and acquire a more varied membership. The basic view of the two religious parties, that politics was not an autonomous field but part of a more comprehensive socioreligious complex, encouraged them to initiate social activity among rural and urban workers. These activities included charity fund-raising campaigns, public discussions on religion and morality, and the delivery of sermons in the mosques.[18] However, despite the three parties' attempts to gain support from broader circles of the population, for the most part they were successful only in urban concentrations and among educated groups there.

The small membership of the three parties is a further indication of the fact that they were based mainly on politically aware groups

16. Sela, "Mifleget ha-ba'th," in "Ha-Miflagot ha-politiyot ba-Gada ha-Ma'aravit," pp. 100–01.

17. Ibid., p. 130.

18. On the extent of the Muslim Brotherhood's social activities, see, for instance, reports of March 28, 1953, June 21, 1959, and May 19, 1962, ISA, File 718–40; Simon, "Ha-Ahim ha-muslemim," in "Ha-Miflagot ha-politiyot ba-Gada ha-Ma'aravit," pp. 304–05. On the Tahrir party's social activities see report of January 23, 1958, ISA, File 439–8; Simon and Landau "Mifleget ha-shihrur," in "Ha-Miflagot ha-politiyot ba-Gada ha-Ma'aravit," p. 428.

and were unable to develop the machinery to recruit new types of members. In the 1960s the membership of al-Tahrir and the Muslim Brotherhood numbered no more than 700, and that of al-Qawmiyyun was even smaller.[19] Most of them were a core of agitators selected to stimulate opposition activity. Amman's suppressive actions made the recruitment of even the educated groups difficult. Some of the party members were economically dependent on the resources of the Jordanian regime. Teachers and civil servants were especially vulnerable to retaliation—the loss of employment—for engaging in opposition activity. Those members who wanted to retain their positions, which they could use to influence the public, had to act carefully and moderately, if at all, so as not to give the authorities a pretext for firing them.

In sum, Amman's control of material resources as well as its preventive actions seriously hurt the opposition parties' ability to develop mass political activity in order to challenge Amman's rule in the West Bank. Most of the time the groups concentrated on setting up organizational frameworks just to keep their parties alive—the question of their survival overruled all other concerns. Material assistance from regimes in Syria and Egypt after the mid-1950s helped some opposition parties, especially the Ba'th and al-Qawmiyyun, to continue their activities under constant Jordanian surveillance.[20] But dependence on external financial aid also reduced the parties' autonomy and increased Amman's ability to control their activity through agreements with other Arab countries. For this reason, Amman's influence on the opposition's attitudes and behavior passed not only through the West Bank but also through some Arab capitals. The scope and intensity of the activity of the opposition groups in the West Bank became a function of inter-Arab politics beyond Palestinian control. It seemed unlikely, therefore, that the opposition parties could independently challenge the rule of Amman in the West Bank.

19. Cohen, "Political Parties in the West Bank," p. 41.
20. On Syrian financial support to Ba'th members in Jordan who were arrested or dismissed from their work by the government, see report of August 26, 1958, ISA, File 425–7; Sela, "Mifleget ha-ba'th," p. 107.

THE LACK OF AN ALL-WEST-BANK LEADERSHIP

Amman's success in retaining control of the loci of power in the West Bank also rested on an administrative structure and policies that limited the opportunities for the creation of an all-West-Bank political framework. The lack of an effective all-West-Bank leadership meant that the Palestinian leaders drew their power mainly from local bases and could not expand it to cover the entire West Bank population. Given the narrow local bases of their economic and social standing, these leaders lacked the political support needed to become national figures. Formal positions on the national Jordanian level, such as seats in the Senate, the House of Representatives, or even the cabinet, did not constitute effective and fully legitimate means of expanding these power bases, partly because of the West Bank public's ambivalence about its own political identity and its relationship to Amman. Furthermore, most of the West Bank political leaders belonged to families with commercial and economic interests, and their property was affected by government policy. Their vulnerability to adverse policy decisions in Amman discouraged them from adopting positions that might lead to an open clash with the rulers of the country.

The inability of Palestinian leaders to continue to use Jerusalem as a focus for a wider power base was the result of a government policy that diminished Jerusalem's status. Under the British Mandate, Jerusalem had been the seat of government, but now Amman was the sole capital.[21] Shortly after annexation the Jordanian regime took steps to underscore Amman's centrality. District administrative offices were made directly responsible to the ministries in Amman, and the Jerusalem offices were given absolutely no authority in the rest of the West Bank.[22] Moreover, the administra-

21. On Jerusalem's status under the British Mandate as a social and political center for the Arabs of Palestine, see Y. Shimoni, '*Arviyey Eretz-Yisra'el* [The Arabs of Palestine] (Tel-Aviv: Am-Oved, 1947), pp. 210–22, 385–88, 393–95.

22. See a decree of December 1949 in *al-Jarida al-Rasmiyya*, December 17, 1949.

tion decided to transfer all government offices to Amman by April 1951.[23]

The Palestinian leadership continually criticized Amman's policy on Jerusalem. "The Jerusalem municipality," wrote M. P. Anwar Nusayba in the early 1950s to the Speaker of the House, "is almost the only one that does not get any aid or encouragement from the government administration. . . . [This] despite the fact that Jerusalem is on the front line of the cities that were struck by the Palestine disaster, and the larger part of the city is held by the invaders. . . . in the eyes of the world, Jerusalem holds a more important place than London or Paris or Washington."[24] Demands were also voiced for turning Jerusalem into a second capital by passing legislation to make it the administrative center of the West Bank, by holding sessions of the House of Representatives there, or by proclaiming it the spiritual and religious capital of the kingdom.[25] Despite the opposition of West Bank representatives and local organizations, such as the Jerusalem City Council, the Supreme Muslim Council, and the Chamber of Commerce, the Jordanian government was determined to transfer the center of governmental gravity from Jerusalem to Amman. Besides depriving the Jerusalem leadership of the advantage it had had under the Mandate of being close to the seat of British administrative power, the downgrading of Jerusalem also tended to increase the possibility that the leadership would be crystallized and strengthened in other local urban centers in the West Bank. The purpose of Amman's policy was to intensify local interests and encourage rivalry among the localities for the resources allocated.

During Jordanian rule in the West Bank, the leadership of Nablus became one of the strongest local elites in the West Bank. After

23. See *Filastin,* November 18, 1950.

24. As cited in Be'eri, "Ma'amada shel Yerushalayim," mimeographed (n.p., n.d.), p. 2. For a letter on the same issue which was sent to the Jordanian cabinet by fourteen West Bank representatives, see *al-Hayat* (Beirut), August 2, 1952.

25. *Filastin,* June 24, 1955; *al-Difa',* November 25, 1954, and February 4, 1955.

Jerusalem, Nablus was considered the most important city in the West Bank. Its importance stemmed from the size of its population, its level of economic development, and the high status of its notable families.[26] From 23,250 on the eve of annexation, Nablus's population grew to 41,537 by 1967, and it became the second largest city on the West Bank.[27] Its commercial and economic development was due mainly to its position as the regional center for the surrounding cities and towns. The lifting of restrictions on movement between the East and the West banks on November 14, 1949, and the abolishment of customs duties on goods going to the East Bank by the decree of December 1, 1949, encouraged trade between the two banks and benefitted Nablus.[28] Amman's resource allocation policy vis-à-vis the West Bank, and Nablus in particular, was never consistent or uniform. The economic and political influence of the traditional notable families there—such as al-Masri, al-Nabulsi, Tuqan, Shak'a, and 'Abd al-Hadi—which was not restricted to the city itself, and their tradition of adopting relatively independent positions helped the city's local elite to gain a special political status in the West Bank as well as in the kingdom.

The southern Hebron leadership was another example of a local elite with special political status in the West Bank. Hebron's population increased from 24,600 before annexation to 38,091 in 1967.[29] While in Nablus light industry and crafts were important, in Hebron the economy was largely agricultural. "More than any other city in Judea and Samaria," as Yehuda Karmon and Avshalom Shmueli argue, "Hebron obtained the character of a traditional Middle Eastern city in which the urban functions are only complementary

26. See Erik Cohen, "He-'Arim ba-shetahim ha-muhzakim" [The cities in the administered territories], mimeographed (Jerusalem: Department of Sociology, The Hebrew University of Jerusalem, 1968), pp. 17–26.

27. See Elisha Efrat, "Hishtanut ma'arakh ha-yishuvim bi-Yehuda w-Shomron, 1947–1967" [Changes in the patterns of settlement in Judea and Samaria, 1947–1967], *HMH* 23 (1973):291.

28. On the abolition of the restrictions see *al-Urdun,* December 1 and 2, 1949; Gadi Zilberman, "Temurot kalkaliyot ba-'ir Shchem ba-shanim, 1949–1967," mimeographed (Institute of African and Asian Studies, The Hebrew University of Jerusalem, 1972), p. 8.

29. Efrat, "Hishtanut ma'arakh ha-yishuvim," p. 291.

to the economy of the community, and agriculture holds pride of place and rules the city landscape."[30] Over half the work force in the city was engaged in agriculture on either a full-time or part-time basis, and 70 percent of the inhabitants owned agricultural land. The particularly high migration rate in the Hebron mountains and the distance from the main roads to the East Bank also helped the city retain its traditional social structure.[31]

The differences between Nablus and Hebron were reflected in the way their leadership operated. While in Nablus there were bitter power struggles within the local leadership, in Hebron there was less fragmentation. The main conflict in Hebron between al-Khatib and al-Ja'bari families was contained, although not solved, by relatively clear-cut divisions of power. Members of al-Khatib family served in the cabinet and the House of Representatives; members of al-Ja'bari family served mainly in high religious positions and in local government.

Ramallah's local elite was also politically influential though less important than those of Nablus and Hebron. Ramallah's uniqueness lay in its Christian background. In 1967 more than half its population of 12,000 was Christian.[32] Moreover, the local elite families were Christian families that had arrived in the area with the beginning of the Ottoman rule in Palestine. Apparently their influence extended beyond the city limits, and some of them played important roles on the national level in Jordan. Jalil Harib of the Yusuf family, for instance, served as minister of the economy and Sam'an Da'ud of the Sharaqa family as minister of justice in the mid-1950s, while 'Isa 'Aql of the Ibrahim family was a member of Parliament.[33]

The composition of Ramallah's population and particularly of its

30. Y. Karmon and A. Shmueli, *Hevron, demuta shel 'ir hararit* [Hebron, face of a mountain city] (Tel-Aviv: Goma, 1970), p. 80.

31. Ibid.

32. Efrat, "Hishtanut ma'arakh ha-yishuvim," p. 291.

33. For details on the structure and major personalities of the different extended families, see Binyamin Shidlovsky, *"Ramallah-al-Birah, Skira Hevratit-Politit"* [Ramallah al-Birah, sociopolitical survey], mimeographed (Judea and Samaria Area Command, 1970), pp. 21–23.

elite had an important effect on the city's politics. The Christian population, notable for its high proportion of educated people, was exposed to radical moods and political influences. Many of the city's citizens were active in leftist political groups, such as the Ba'th and the Communist party. The impact of Ramallah's Christian character on its political life becomes even more striking when one compares it to the neighboring Muslim city of al-Birah, which had about the same population. Muslim al-Birah made a much smaller impression on West Bank political life than Ramallah. The important role that the local leadership in Ramallah, Nablus, and Hebron played in West Bank politics in the 1950s and 1960s suited the Jordanian administration's policy of preventing Jerusalem from becoming a political focus or administrative center for the entire West Bank.

The system of elections to the House of Representatives and the Jordanian Municipal Elections Law, which permitted the Jordanian central authorities to influence the election results, was also used by the government to strengthen parochial-local interests against all–West-Bank aspirations. For the purpose of elections to the House of Representatives, the West Bank was divided into seven constituencies that elected half the members of the house; these were Jerusalem-Jericho, Hebron, Nablus, Ramallah, Bethlehem, Tulkarm, and Jenin. The election law stated that a candidate's victory was determined by the proportion of the total vote cast for him, in accordance with the number of deputies allocated to each region.

The system of seven constituencies seems to have helped Amman to obtain the election of the candidates it wanted more than a proportional representation system would have done. The latter system would have forced the pro-Jordanian parties to campaign along a wider front and lessened their chances of success. This theory seems to be supported by the electoral defeats of the opposition Ba'th, al-Qawmiyyun, and al-Tahrir parties, which could run legally in some elections and in others had candidates who fronted for them.

In the first elections to the House of Representatives after annexation, in April 1950, candidates who held Ba'thist and Communist views won only two seats each out of thirty, while al-Tahrir and the Muslim Brotherhood did not win even one. On the other hand, a pro-Jordanian party, Hizb al-Dusturi al-'arabi (the Arab Constitutional party), won eight seats and al-Umma (the National party) two. Al-Hizb al-Watani al-Ishtiraki (the National Socialist party) won ten seats in that election, but, it should be recalled, it expressed rather more moderate views in those days compared to the mid-1950s.[34] The composition of the House of Representatives revealed a striking number of West Bank members who supported the regime. Most of them had local power bases stemming from their family status. Opposition figures such as Na'was and al-Rimawi of the Ba'th party present a stark contrast; they usually lacked a local power base.

The second parliamentary elections in late August 1951 produced a party distribution only slightly different from the first one. The Ba'thists gained one seat, for a total of three. The Communists retained their two seats. Al-Tahrir and the Muslim Brotherhood were again left with no representatives in the house. Al-Hizb al-Dusturi increased its representation from eight to nine seats and the National Socialist party from ten to eleven. The Umma party representation was reduced from two seats to one.[35]

In the third parliamentary elections in mid-October 1954, the opposition parties' defeat was total. The Ba'thists' intensive campaign and the generous assistance they received from Syria and Egypt did not pay off, and they lost their seats. Al-Hizb al-Dusturi almost doubled its representation, from eight seats to seventeen. Some of the opposition parties boycotted the elections, accusing the authorities of interfering with the electoral process.

To insure its authority, Amman manipulated the party system with respect to representation of the two banks in Parliament. First, the party system was structured to overrepresent the more sparsely populated constituencies on the East Bank and limit the influence of the populous constituencies on the West Bank. In the 1950s, for example, the Jerusalem district, with a population

34. For more details see Kamel S. Abu Jaber, "The Jordanian Parliament," in *Man, State, and Society in the Contemporary Middle East*, ed. Jacob M. Landau (New York: Praeger, 1972), p. 99.

35. Ibid., p. 101.

of 150,000, and Ramallah, with 120,000, were represented by three members while the southern district of Transjordan, which included Kerak, Ma'an, and Tafila, had five members, although its population was only about 90,000. Second, Amman structured the system to overrepresent constituents in the West Bank whose support of the regime was certain. The more sympathetic and loyal the inhabitants of the constituency were to the regime the more seats they were allotted in Parliament. Thus the Hebron district, with a population of 135,000 and known for its loyalty to the regime, was represented by four members, as was the Nablus district, with a population of 175,000.[36]

The regime also influenced elections by giving soldiers the right to vote wherever they were stationed on the day of the election. This regulation was particularly important in the first three elections, when a force of about 10,000 men was located in the West Bank. Even General John Glubb, referring in his memoirs to the elections to the Third Parliament, admitted that the names of progovernment candidates were marked on the lists given to the soliders at the polls.[37]

Amman also tried to influence elections for the local and municipal councils in order to keep opposition groups from challenging its policies. The 1955 Municipal Law stated that the area of jurisdiction of a municipality constituted a single electoral district. The minister of the interior, however, reserved the right to split it into several districts and to determine the boundaries of the districts and the number of members each would elect to the municipal council. Moreover, the central authorities had the right to appoint two members to the municipal council in addition to those elected by the voters and to appoint the mayor. On October 18, 1964, for instance, the minister of the interior appointed a long-time

36. See *HMH* 1 (1950):214–15.

37. John Bagot Glubb, *A Soldier with the Arabs* (London: Hedder and Stoughton, 1957), p. 351. Glubb claims, however, that no attempt was made to convince them to choose any particular candidate, although "It is possible that a number of soldiers voted for Taufiq Pasha's men when they saw them marked as 'Government Candidates.'"

Hashemite supporter, Sheikh Muhammad 'Ali al-Ja'bari, to the Hebron City Council and to the office of mayor.[38]

Another way in which the government influenced the elections was by determining who could vote and could not vote. The Municipal Elections Law restricted suffrage to persons who paid a "land or any municipal tax at a rate of at least one dinar during the twelve consecutive months preceding the election, on condition that if the property is held by more than one resident each of the property holders pays his share."[39] As a result, only men with property or capital or in possession of some asset for which they paid taxes could vote. The more traditional property owners thus dominated the voting list. If they paid the tax for their tenants, they assured the right of the latter to vote and thus extended support for the candidates they favored through voters outside their immediate family or religious group. In this way, the tendency for candidates' lists to allot representation to the various families in the municipality strengthened parochial-local interests and limited the probability that opposition figures would be successful in appealing to the electorate as all-West-Bank leaders.

If we trace the lists of candidates for municipal elections in the West Bank in the 1950s and 1960s we find that the *hamula,* or extended family, always tended to present the same candidates as part of a division of positions of power among the *hamula* heads. Thus Hajj M'azuz al-Masri was elected to the Nablus municipal council in three of the four elections from 1951 to 1967, while Hikmat al-Masri sat for Nablus in the House of Representatives. Similarly, 'Adil al-Shak'a sat on the Nablus municipal council throughout the entire period of Jordanian rule in the West Bank, while Walid al-Shak'a was active on the national level as a member

38. Fore more details see Ori Stendel, *Ha-Behirot la-'iriyot ba-Gada ha-Ma'aravit (1951–1967)* [The municipal election in the West Bank (1951–1957], mimeographed (Judea and Samaria Area Command, 1968), pp. 2–3.

39. Article 12, as cited in Ibid., p. 6. The other conditions were that the voter be a male Jordanian citizen, aged 21, resident in the area of jurisdiction of the municipality during the twelve months prior to the preparation of the electoral list, and sane.

of the House of Representatives from 1951 to 1956. The same trend is apparent in other cities. Under these circumstances candidates who were not of landowning families did not stand much chance even if they had other assets, such as education or a profession. Even when the trend for young educated men to run for office merged in the 1960s the new candidates tended to be young educated members of families with high status and prestige. In Ramallah, for instance, the young and educated Nadim Zaru, a candidate of the 'Awwad *hamula,* one of the oldest families in the city, became a city councillor in 1964. In short, limited change permitted a different type of leader to be chosen without undermining the traditional patterns of local authority centered on the prestigious *hamulas.*[40] Acquisition of power through a formal position in the government continued largely to be at the pleasure of the political establishment in Amman.

Only in the 1956 election campaign was there a serious attempt by West Bank opposition parties to turn Parliament into a source of real political power. This was perhaps the only election in which the Amman authorities did not intervene blatantly, and consequently the elected Parliament, not the court, constituted the major power base for Prime Minister Sulayman al-Nabulsi's cabinet. The dismissal of the cabinet in April 1957 and the dissolution of Parliament indicated the court's fear of losing control of the loci of power and its fear of an all–West-Bank opposition leadership. The court expressed these fears further by taking a hard line against the opposition, as we have seen.

Lacking West-Bank–wide authority, local West Bank leaders tended to operate as interest groups attempting to influence Amman's allocation of resources rather than as integral components of the decision-making process. Both the pro-Jordanian West Bank leaders and those who were inclined toward opposition activity tended to act more as brokers between the Palestinian population and the rulers in Amman or the Arab regimes than as equal Arab partners. It is true that Palestinians played ministerial as well as parliamentary roles in Jordan, but policy, especially on sensitive issues, was the

40. See Shidlovshy, "Ramallah-al-Birah," pp. 62–63.

province of small circles in the Jordanian administration composed almost exclusively of East Bankers of Transjordanian or Palestinian origin. Only on the local level–and even there only to the extent that resources were actually controlled by municipal authorities, local chambers of commerce, and voluntary welfare organizations— could the West Bank leadership truly be said to have had some control over the allocation of resources.

By concentrating on material benefits and day-to-day activities, the pro-Jordanian leadership in the West Bank denied itself the role of national leadership representing the political symbols of the Palestinian community. This leadership, though, was not really in a position to fulfill the solidary-national function; its limited legitimacy was based mostly on the social structure of local communities and not on more integrative nationalist values or structures. In some respects the national leadership's functions were performed by non-Palestinian Arab leaders with pan-Arab ambitions such as President Nasir and 'Abd al-Karim Qasim, particularly as the Egyptian and Iraqi mass media overcame geographical distance to arouse Arab national solidarity outside their own borders. It is true, all the same, that during periods of unrest in the West Bank, there emerged a Palestinian political leadership comprised of young educated men, many of whom had received their schooling in other Arab countries. This leadership was ideologically articulate and held radical social and nationalistic views. In the main, however, it tended to enhance popular identification with the pan-Arab political leadership rather than lead to the development of a national leadership in its own right.

The weakness of a leadership comprised of educated men lay in its inability to draw power either from its institutional or its socioeconomic status. Nor, given the lack of meaningful party activity, could it find effective channels for participation in the existing Jordanian political system. The only route open to an energetic national leadership, then, lay underground, inside or outside Jordan, in Palestinian or other radical bodies. The existence of this route, moreover, to some extent relieved the pressure for elite rotation in the West Bank, where the pattern of local and day-to-day political life continued to prevail.

During most of the 1950s and 1960s Amman remained in a stable position of power, because the regime prevented the Palestinian opposition from building an alternative power base. Amman's policies perpetuated the weak organizational structures of the opposition parties and limited their recruitment of support from broad circles of the Palestinian population. Amman's ability to retain control over the Palestinians was due to its manipulative policies, particularly its structuring of the electoral system, which carefully restricted Palestinian participation in national decision-making and prevented the formation of an all–West-Bank leadership. Furthermore, Amman was helped by the fact that the Palestinian opposition had to pay a political price for accepting political support from outside the kingdom in order to attain its political ends. The Palestinians had to shape their objectives and modes of operation to fit those of the radical Arab regimes as well as to take into account changes in the relations of those regimes with Amman. This explains why the radical Palestinian slogan of the mid-1960s— that the road to regain Palestine passes through Amman—remained a political dream.

6

Conclusion:
Coexistence in Protracted Conflict

Nineteen sixty-four was the year of the formation of the Palestine Liberation Organization (PLO). The organization, which was recognized by the Arab countries, including Jordan, sought to hold its first congress in the Old City of Jerusalem. Jordan, seeking a less emotion-laden site, proposed Amman, which the Palestinians rejected. Then Jordan suggested Qalia on the shores of the Dead Sea, probably as a hint that the congress might die before it began. This proposal was fiercely rejected. A compromise was finally reached; the congress was held at the Intercontinental Hotel, near Mount Scopus in Jerusalem but *not* in the Old City.[1]

"Common sense," as Molière put it, "avoids extremes." This is what set the tone among the Palestinians and in Amman and prevented crisis. One might interpret the dispute over the PLO congress as a case of total conflict of interest leading inevitably to confrontation. For Amman and the Palestinians, however, it was instead a case of compromise typical of their coexistence in a situation of protracted conflict. As we have seen, this form of coexistence persisted throughout most of the period between 1949 and 1967. The ways in which patterns of conditional legitimacy, floating identity, and power relations contained conflict between Amman and the Palestinians during this period are relevant to an understanding of West Bank politics after the 1967 war and to other situations of protracted conflict between political communities.

1. See Ahmad al-Shuqayri, *Min al-qimma ila al-hazima ma' al-muluk wa al-rua'sa'* (Beirut: Dar al-'Awda, 1971), p. 96.

CONFLICT WITHIN COEXISTENCE, 1949–67

After the annexation of the West Bank by Jordan, the basic political desires guiding the Palestinians and the Jordanian regime seldom coincided. Recovery of Palestine from the Jews and the establishment of Palestinian or Arab rule over the entire territory of Palestine became the central political dream of many Palestinians. Amman, on the other hand, sought to gain the loyalty of and control over the Palestinians in order to integrate the West Bank into the Kingdom of Jordan. Paradoxically, their conflicting desires and the political and ideological circumstances encouraged both sides to cooperate with each other. Most of the time Amman and political groups among the Palestinians preferred at least some conciliation to violent confrontation and minimal collaboration to fatal collision. Both sides tended to opt for arrangements that balanced the pressures of conflict against their interest in cooperation. They realized that the price each would have to pay in order to fulfill its aims through one-sided solutions was unacceptably high.

The tendencies toward moderation of conflict and strengthening of cooperation between Amman and the West Bank derived from a mutual need. The social and cultural advantages of the West Bank population over the East Bank as well as its political connections with Arab regimes outside Jordan gave the Palestinian leaders some leverage with Amman. However, the West Bank's lower geopolitical status after annexation and Jordan's monopoly of both military and economic power balanced this advantage. The Palestinians on the West Bank could not act independently. The dialogue between the two banks became a way of life.

The dialogue between Amman and the West Bank was sustained by a common inclination to avoid clear definitions of their collective boundaries. The absence of a clear definition derived, as in other Arab communities, from simultaneous awareness on the part of both Palestinians and Jordanians of two primordial Arab allegiances. One was that of *qawmiyya*, an abstract noun from *qawm*, meaning people, group, or tribe, used to express political allegiance and commitment of social units to the realization of Arab nationalism through unity. The second was that of *wataniyya*, from *watan*, which means country or homeland and expresses patriotic attachment to a single country.[2]

Palestinian attachment to *qawmiyya* and *wataniyya,* or broad nationalism and narrow patriotism, permitted political groups in the West Bank to define their collective identity in pan-Arab, pan-Islamic, Palestinian, or Jordanian terms without committing themselves to the central symbols of either the Jordanian or other Arab regimes. They were Palestinians, and at the same time they were Jordanians, and they relied heavily on pan-Arab and pan-Islamic symbols. The name of the largest guerrilla organization, Fatah, for instance, means in Arabic a conquest for Islam gained in the Holy War, and the three brigades of the Palestinian Liberation Army—Qadisiyya, Hittin, and 'Ayn Jalut—were named after great victories won by Muslim arms.[3]

The absence among the Paestinians of a clear definition of their collective identity was similar to Amman's ambiguity about the content of Jordanian identity. Some political circles in Amman did not accept the finality of Jordan's political boundaries. King 'Adballah had for many years seen the realization of the Hashemites' political dream in "Greater Syria," which would include Syria, Lebanon, Palestine, and Transjordan. By sharing a similar ambivalence with the Palestinians about the definition of their collective identity and political boundaries, Amman left room for various possibilities of ideological cooperation, even with its Palestinian rivals.

Cooperation was fostered by Amman's declarations that Jordan's political objectives were identical with those of the Palestinians, especially on issues such as the restoration of Palestine, the struggle

2. For more on these terms see Sati' al-Husri *Al-'Uruba awwalan* [Arabism first] (Beirut: Dar al-'ilm lil-malayin, 1955) p. 13. For a detailed analysis see Sylvia G. Haim, "Islam and the Theory of Arab Nationalism," in *The Middle East in Transition,* ed. Walter Z. Laqueur (London: Routledge and Kegan Paul, 1958), pp. 287–98.

3. See Bernard Lewis, "The Return of Islam," *Commentary* 61 (1976):42. "It is hardly surprising"—writes Lewis—"that the military communiqués of the Fatah begin with the Muslim invocation, 'In the name of God, the Merciful and the Compassionate.'"

against colonialism, and the desire for Arab unity. On these issues, Amman's expressed ultimate political objectives coincided with those of the Palestinians as well as with those of other Arab countries. The differences between the parties were, as presented by Amman, artificial, temporary, and bound to disappear in the long run when the Arabs' final goals were realized. This distinction between temporary and ultimate goals—the short and the long run—enabled the regime in Amman to carry out a policy that was in fact incompatible with the Palestinians' political goals. Until the 1967 war for instance, the Jordanian regime drew a careful and very fine distinction between Palestine as an Arab land and the Palestinians as a political community. "Liberation of Palestine" as an all-Arab issue was considered a matter for long-run policy. But the Jordanians could not easily accept "liberation of the Palestinians." This would only have enhanced the sense of difference and exacerbated tensions between the Palestinians and Jordan.[4]

King Hussein explicity articulated this distinction in 1965, when he declared that he regarded Palestine as the ultimate goal, but "the organizations which seek to separate Palestinians from Jordanians are traitors helping Zionism in its aim of undermining the Arab camp."[5] Amman thus preferred to talk of routing out the enemies of Arab nationalism while suppressing enemies of the regime; of arresting Communists and traitors while seizing PLO and Fatah members and supporters. In sum, the regime in Amman maintained its control over the loci of power in the context of coexistence by justifying its policy toward the Palestinians in broad terms of Arab unity; most of the time it preferred not to take an unequivocal and firm position against its Palestinian rivals. It controlled the Palestinians not only through its use of material resources but also through its ability to manipulate the meaning of Palestinian desires, thus limiting the political options open to the Palestinians. This ability became its secret weapon.

Amman's approach did not prevent Palestinian political groups,

4. When the West Bank came under Israeli occupation in 1967 it became much easier for Amman to fuse the terms "Palestine" and "Palestinians."
5. As cited in *al-Watha'iq al-filastiniyya li-'am 1966* (Beirut: The Institute for Palestine Studies, 1967), document no. 125, p. 303.

both moderate and hard-line, from criticizing the regime on domestic as well as foreign policy issues. They were even involved, passively and actively, in anti-Jordanian acts. For most of the years between 1949 and 1967, however, Palestinian political groups did not take an approach of total opposition toward Amman. The conflict was perceived more as an intermediate situation of prolonged tension and contradictions to be dealt with by mitigating the antagonism rather than trying to solve it. In this respect, most of the political groups in the West Bank avoided adopting clear-cut political doctrines regarding relations with Amman and opted instead for patterns of temporary accommodation like conditional legitimacy and floating identity that persisted for a relatively long time. Moroever, it seems that the prolonging of coexistence between the two banks fostered patterns of relations in which *recognition of the transitoriness of the arrangements paradoxically contributed to their persistence.*

The perception of arrangements as temporary had two aspects. On the one hand, it reflected the feeling of political groups in the West Bank that they were engaged in an unresolved conflict. It thus entailed nonacceptance of the Jordanian political order at least in terms of ultimate goals. On the other hand, it made it possible for Palestinian political circles to reconcile themselves to the situation in the short run until they acquired the means for realizing their goals. The perception of arrangements as temporary thus offered not only the potential for change but also the possibility of maintaining the Jordanian political order. By regarding their political existence under Jordanian rule as temporary, the Palestinian opposition could put off confronting Amman over issues that had high potential for immediate conflict, such as the question of its political identity and the nature of long-term relations between the two banks.

To cope with the anomaly of their political position, in most of the years of Jordanian rule in the West Bank the Palestinians were willing to accept a certain degree of ambiguity both in the definition of their political goals and in the attribution of any symbolic meaning to their practical accomplishments under Jordanian rule. The operative meaning of such terms as territory, sovereignty, and national leadership, which were common in the West Bank in the first years after its incorporation into Jordan, became increasingly ambiguous and tied to the mobilization of all Arab resources. At the same time, daily politics were carried on by local leaders lacking the ability and legitimacy to establish themselves on an all-West-Bank basis. Palestinian leaders in the West Bank therefore became an object for manipulation by Amman rather than an independent political element controlling their own resources. Under some circumstances Palestinian local leaders were even willing to use the most suitable definition of their political identity—Palestinian, Arab, Muslim, or Jordanian—to improve their bargaining position with Amman or with other Arab regimes.

In most of the years 1949–67 relations between West Bank Palestinians and Amman were characterized neither by increasing integration nor by a heightening of conflict to outright confrontation but by delicately contained conflict. This relationship contradicts less nuanced generalizations such as T. E. Lawrence's statement that "Semites had no half-tones in their register of vision. . . . They never compromised: they pursued the logic of several incompatible opinions to absurd ends."[6]

POST-1967: CHANGE OR CONTINUITY?

The emergence of radical Palestinian groups outside the West Bank a few years before the 1967 war, particularly around Palestinian intellectuals in Lebanon and around the Fatah guerrilla organization, constituted a serious challenge to the willingness of political groups in the West Bank to accept coexistence through acquiescence in temporary arrangements. In order to restore the Palestinians to a central role in the political and military struggle for Palestine, the radicals sought to bypass the temporary arrangements and focus attention on a solution to the problem of Palestine. One can also argue that, paradoxically, the Israeli victory in the 1967 war helped the radical Palestinians by shifting the emphasis of Arab concerns in Palestine from ultimate and long-run to more operational and short-run. The separation of the West Bank from Jordanian control

6. T. E. Lawrence, *Seven Pillars of Wisdom: A Triumph* (New York: Garden City Publishing, 1938), p. 38.

thus undermined the temporary political arrangements that had been the basis for coexistence. The Palestinian desire to force the Israelis out of the West Bank necessitated a radical change in the political and territorial status quo, which was perceived as potentially opening up options for Palestinian sovereignty in the West Bank.

The push for radical change, however, was balanced by several factors: the collaboration between Jordan and Israel that was epitomized by the policy of "open bridges" across the Jordan River after the 1967 war, growing cooperation between the local West Bank leadership and the Israeli military government, and the hope held by some Palestinians on the West Bank that Amman would help them extricate themselves from Israeli rule. All these factors contributed to the continuity of temporary arrangements as the preferred solution for most of the Palestinians in the West Bank. They continued to play a significant role in the political relations of the West Bank with Israel, Jordan, and the PLO.

After the 1967 war, local leaders in the West Bank, as under the Jordanian regime, preferred to focus on daily politics in their relationship with the Israeli military government, which was considered a temporary ruler. At the same time Palestinian national leadership functions continued to be performed by Palestinian or Arab bodies outside the West Bank. This distinction between daily and national political functions helped the local leaders to regard the political future of the West Bank as an issue for negotiation between Israel and political elements outside the West Bank rather than between themselves and the Israeli authorities. It helped the West Bank leaders to avoid making clear-cut decisions regarding Israel, Jordan, or the PLO and upsetting their delicate relations with each of these parties.

It is true that during the first months after the 1967 war some attempts were made by West Bank Palestinian leaders to carry on a dialogue with the Israelis about the possibilities for a political solution. It was reported, for example, that thirty notables were ready to sign a formal declaration of political cooperation with Israel provided the Israeli government accepted the idea of establishing a Palestinian state on the West Bank. Apart from a few such incidents, however, this kind of political initiative declined and became very sporadic.[7] Political attempts by the West Bank leaders to deal with Israel about a political solution for the West Bank could undermine the internal conflict among themselves regarding the desired settlement and aggravate the Israelis, who were determined to negotiate with Amman on the future of the West Bank.

Radical politics expressed in demands for an ultimate solution did not become the main activity of the West Bank's Palestinian leadership. Daily relations between the Israeli authorities and this leadership continued, even during periods of riots and demonstrations. The pattern of day-to-day cooperation coincided not only with the self-interest of West Bank leaders and of Israel but also with that of Amman and the PLO. Both Amman and the PLO sought to prevent local political initiatives that could limit their influence on the West Bank's political future.

The principal instrument for the maintenance of Jordanian influence on the West Bank was the distribution of money payments to Palestinians who were loyal to the Jordanian authorities. The latter attempted by means of these payments to prevent cooperation between the local leadership and Israeli officials. Since 1970, however, the Jordanian government has reconciled itself to the situation of current daily contact between the Israeli authorities and the West Bank's mayors and notables. From Amman's point of view, these contacts did not undermine its influence in the West Bank as long as the Israeli government did not negotiate with the West Bank leaders or with the PLO on the future of the West Bank.

Jordanian policy toward the West Bank can be seen as an outcome of a growing understanding between Israel and Jordan based on the distinction between daily political matters for which Israel felt it should be directly responsible and more fundamental issues about which the Jordanians were particularly sensitive. This relationship helped the local leadership to continue to focus on daily events and avoid responsibility for broader political issues. Mayors and other local leaders in the West Bank who did not adjust to this trend encountered difficulties and lost their positions. This was the

7. For more details on these attempts, see Mark Allan Heller, "Foreign Occupation and Political Elites: A Study of the Palestinians," (Ph.D. diss., Harvard University, 1976), pp. 288–30.

case with Hamdi Kan'an, mayor of Nablus, who sought to turn his position into regional and even national leadership, and Nadim Zaru, mayor of Ramallah, who was known for his radical nationalist views. Their initiative was not consistent with the nature of local leadership activity or with the political interests of Israel and Jordan.

The West Bank leaders' tendency to concentrate on day-to-day activity as against taking political initiatives also coincided to some extent with the PLO's political interest in the West Bank. The PLO claimed that it—not Amman or leaders living under Israeli rule—was the authoritative representative of the Palestinians of the West Bank. The acceptance of this argument by the West Bank leaders, whether for ideological or tactical reasons, emphasized their lack of direct involvement in dealing with a final solution for the West Bank.

The local leadership's ability to maintain a balance between the conflicting interests of Israel, Jordan, and the PLO by focusing on daily politics and relying on temporary arrangements began to wane after 1973 as the PLO began to achieve a high level of recognition in Arab as well as in international forums. This development strengthened the belief among broad sectors of the West Bank population that the PLO, not Amman, would be successor to the Israelis. In the eyes of many West Bankers the possibility of a Palestinian state on the West Bank looked brighter than it had in the past. The PLO's elevated position in West Bank eyes was reflected in the 1976 municipal election results. As in the 1972 elections, individuals with a radical view who did not belong to the traditional local leadership attempted to fill the political vacuum created by the focus of this leadership on daily activity. While most of these candidates failed to obtain any significant gains in the 1972 municipal elections, they showed impressive success in 1976. The mayors of the two largest cities, Nablus and Hebron, and the landlords and businessmen who served as members of governing councils in many municipalities were replaced by blue-collar workers, some of whom were connected with radical parties like the Ba'th and the Communists, or by PLO supporters.[8]

8. For a discussion of the election results see Ibid., pp. 274–89; also Michael Walzer, "Israeli Policy and the West Bank," *Dissent* (Summer 1976), pp. 234–36.

Many observers called the election results a turning point in the West Bank's relations with Israel and Amman. However, the newly elected leaders, especially the new mayors of Nablus and Hebron, continued to behave like their predecessors: they concentrated on day-to-day activity, justifying it as a temporary arrangement, rather than on taking political initiative beyond these contacts. The civil war in Lebanon during 1976 and 1977, as well as the rapprochement between Syria and Jordan, probably encouraged this conservative style of behavior and prevented PLO supporters in the West Bank from trying to take advantage of the new political development. From this standpoint, the transition from Jordanian to Israeli rule occurred in a way that stressed continuity rather than change in the basic Palestinian political pattern of temporary accommodation in the West Bank.

In conclusion, one sees that political communities can find ways to persist even if they are unable to resolve basic conflicts that concern the essence of their existence. They can rely on temporary arrangements, such as accepting the status quo for the short run, and can emphasize patterns of floating identity and conditional legitimacy. These patterns can endure and allow groups to live with and contain political conflict for a long time. But tensions and differences, even if unarticulated, will remain. Ahmad al-Shuqayri, the first chairman of the PLO, demonstrated the Palestinian capacity for living with conflict when he wrote in his memoirs after a meeting with King Hussein at the first Arab summit conference in 1964: "I embraced and kissed King Hussein, and each of us spoke with two tongues about the Palestinian entity."[9]

9. Al-Shuqayri, *Min al-qimma ila al-hazima*, p. 51.

Index

121